Attention and Cognition

This volume explores the psychology of attention and discusses the various cognitive processes that determine what we pay attention to.

Much of our conscious experience is spent interacting with visual objects that we attend to and integrate into our consciousness. This book examines how we navigate this complex world of real and virtual objects, and provides a comprehensive overview of the concept of attention and cognition. It focuses on themes related to different aspects of attention, such as visual cognition and spatial orienting, selection history, priority map, the role of consciousness in attention research, and distractor suppression. It also discusses issues related to forming a comprehensive taxonomy of attention, emerging trends in attention research today and how they are being consolidated into the existing knowledge.

Based on empirical research, this book will be of interest to students, researchers and teachers of cognitive psychology, cognitive science, cognitive and computational neuroscience, and computer sciences. It will also be useful to academicians, psychologists, neuroscientists, mental health professionals and counsellors.

Ramesh Kumar Mishra is a professor at the Centre for Neural and Cognitive Sciences, School of Medical Sciences, University of Hyderabad, India.

Seema Prasad is a postdoctoral fellow in the Cognitive Neurophysiology group, Department of Child and Adolescent Psychiatry, Faculty of Medicine, TU Dresden, Germany.

Attention and Cognition

Current Issues and Recent Approaches

Edited by
Ramesh Kumar Mishra and Seema Prasad

Routledge
Taylor & Francis Group
LONDON AND NEW YORK

First published 2025
by Routledge
4 Park Square, Milton Park, Abingdon, Oxon OX14 4RN

and by Routledge
605 Third Avenue, New York, NY 10158

Routledge is an imprint of the Taylor & Francis Group, an informa business

British Library Cataloguing-in-Publication Data
A catalogue record for this book is available from the British Library

ISBN: 978-1-032-29179-6 (hbk)
ISBN: 978-1-032-42037-0 (pbk)
ISBN: 978-1-003-36089-6 (ebk)

DOI: 10.4324/9781003360896

Typeset in Sabon
by Taylor & Francis Books

Contents

Illustrations

Figures

Tables

Contributors

Brian A. Anderson is Professor of Psychological & Brain Sciences and holds the Carles Puryear Professorship in Liberal Arts at Texas A&M University, USA. He received his Ph.D. from Johns Hopkins University in 2014. He has been recognized with early career awards from the Psychonomic Society, Vision Sciences Society, Association for Psychological Science, and the American Psychological Association.

Soazig Casteau is an Assistant Professor in Psychology at Durham University, her research interests involve studies of the human oculomotor system using both behavioural/eye-tracking and neurostimulation (TMS) methods. In her research, she investigates the interaction between low-level visual processes (e.g., stimuli luminance, location ...), higher level cognitive processes (e.g., attention, memory ...) and oculomotor processes. The aim of her research is to further the understanding of the underlying processes guiding eye movements in simple and complex visual scenes.

Bernhard Hommel (www.bernhard-hommel.eu), now a full professor at Shandong Normal University, China worked previously at Leiden University and the Max-Planck Institute for Psychological Research. He is a member/senator of the German National Academy of Sciences (Leopoldina). His research focuses on cognitive, affective, computational, developmental, social, and neurochemical mechanisms of human and robotic attention and action control.

Haena Kim is a postdoctoral scholar at the University of Chicago, USA. Her research focuses on how past experience influences cognitive processes like attention, decision making and response selection, with a particular focus on aversive learning.

Raymond Klein is a Professor Emeritus at Department of Psychology and Neuroscience, Dalhousie University, Canada. He has been interested in "how the mind works" since beginning graduate school when, working with Michael Posner, he began to become a leading expert on the concept of attention, which is at the nexus of this challenging question. Perhaps best known for his basic research on attention, he has a long-standing interest in applying his knowledge to help solve real-world problems."

Dominique Lamy is a Professor of Psychology and head of the Cognitive psychology program at Tel-Aviv University, Israel. Her research focuses on visual attention and visual awareness. In particular, she investigates the functional differences between conscious and unconscious visual processing and the contributions of stimulus-driven, goal-directed and implicit memory factors to the allocation of attentional priority.

Siobhan McAteer completed her Bachelors in Psychology at Durham University in 2018, before obtaining a Masters in Psychological Research from Oxford University, where she worked with Prof. Masud Husain on distractor filtering in visual working memory. Following this experience, she was awarded funding from Economic and Social Research Council to pursue a PhD at Durham University examining the role of the oculomotor system in visual and spatial working memory under the supervision of Prof Daniel T Smith, which she completed in 2023.

Ramesh Kumar Mishra is a professor at the Centre for Neural and Cognitive Sciences, School of Medical Sciences, University of Hyderabad, India. His professional expertise is in cognitive sciences and allied disciplines. He has published widely in the areas of attention, visual processing, bilingualism and language processing, literacy and its influence on cognition among others. He has edited or authored several books in these areas. His most recent book titled *Bilingualism and Cognitive Control* was published by Springer.

Vaishnavi Mohite has a PhD in Cognitive Sciences, from the University of Hyderabad and is currently a Postdoc at IISC, Bangalore, India. Her research focuses on questions such as: How do we find goal-relevant objects? How does interaction with objects affect how we see them? Can we identify and ignore distractors? How do individuals differ in object perception and selection?

Seema Prasad is a Maria Reiche postdoctoral fellow in the Cognitive Neurophysiology group, Department of Child and Adolescent Psychiatry, Faculty of Medicine, TU Dresden, Germany. She is interested in understanding why humans attend to seemingly irrelevant information. She is examining by looking at curiosity and how it affects attention and cognitive control.

Aniruddha Ramgir is a PhD candidate in the Psychology department of Tel Aviv University, Israel. He explores how previous experience with our visual environment biases what we will attend to next. His research focuses on how we learn to avoid distraction from irrelevant objects that stand out in the environment.

Daniel T. Smith is Professor of Psychology at Durham University. His fundamental research examines the interaction between the motor system, specifically the oculomotor system, and cognitive processes such as attention, working memory. His translational research applies these findings to the understanding, diagnosis and rehabilitation of visual field defects such a hemianopia and neurodegenerative diseases such as Progressive Supranuclear Palsy (PSP).

Daniel Toledano is a PhD candidate in the Psychology department of Tel Aviv University, Israel. He explores how previous experience with our visual environment biases what we will attend to next. His research focuses on the mechanisms underlying the strong attentional bias, by which our attention is preferentially directed towards locations that were previously attended.

1 Introduction

Ramesh Kumar Mishra and Seema Prasad

The human mind has evolved to project meaning onto seemingly meaningless things around us. This assumption has been a part of various schools of philosophy for a long time. To empirically ground the mind, cognitive psychologists have been studying the so-called *cognitive systems* and their behavioral attributes in humans at least since the cognitive revolution. Attention has emerged as the most studied system and now stands on the verge of explaining much higher cognitive phenomena, such as awareness and consciousness. One typical attribute of the attentive mind/brain is that it finds things and accords meanings to them which we then call *cognition*. This process is spontaneous, natural and demonstrable. Although it is a persuasive idea that things are made of features and specialized neurons process such features, we may never know how we still end up "knowing" the very substance and essence of the "thing" in itself or even from its point of view. But most would argue that such metaphysical skepticism may not help in truly appreciating the vast empirical successes of the last few decades in visual cognition, and may be unnecessary.

Within the enterprise of cognitive psychology, most researchers have studied why we attend to the things we do as a typical interplay of attention and the mind of the agent which allows basic cognition. Based on tightly controlled, rigidly executed experimental paradigms, attention experts have proposed models and theories of various kinds that attempt to explain how human attention works. The very act of visual perception and interpretation together constitute a major dimension of cognition. Then, there are individual cultural and biological differences, how all of us fare at it. In sum, empirical progress in visual cognition has revealed a potential door to study the mind in humans, in tasks that they do to survive all the time. This edited volume has gathered some chapters from some of the influential researchers in this field, which are loosely on this theme. How our minds find things and interpret them gives us this holistic phenomenality of meaning and comprehension of the world and the objects in it. A mechanistic explanation of how we attend to some things among others is very important, and has far-reaching implications.

The idea for putting together such a book sprang from the International Symposium on Recent Advances in Attention and Cognition organized by University of Hyderabad in April 2021. It was a virtual conference held during the

DOI: 10.4324/9781003360896-1

Covid-19 pandemic, where we invited some of the finest practitioners of this craft. The speakers were invited to deliver long-format lectures on their core ideas and experimental demonstrations. Many also presented ongoing work at the laboratories on those themes. The lectures provoked interesting discussions afterwards which triggered the motivation to bring out an edited volume based on the themes discussed in the symposium. We then invited several of the original speakers and some new researchers to write comprehensive narratives on their topics that are more elaborate and detailed than the regular journal articles. Some of the speakers could not accept our invitation due to several reasons. However, we succeeded in getting some very strong chapters by leading researchers with a strong presence in the field. Since visual cognition is a very dynamic field, with theories and methods changing swiftly, it is important to document the current trends as well as the ideas that have endured over the years. All of our contributors have done so with their expansive writing and timely presentation of data to back up any speculation. Although we could not assemble many chapters in comparison to many typical edited volumes in this field, whatever we could get is substantive and thematically coherent.

In this collection, many researchers have focused on both top-down and bottom-up aspects of attention. At times, the paradigms and the tasks used may seem too simplistic or even too artificial. However, recurrent findings on such tasks have cemented theories in this domain. Humans keep features of objects that they want to find in their working memory and also actively inhibit those features and entire objects that they don't want to find. This tug of war may seem unconscious to us, but attention does the trick. There are many other examples in this vast domain of research activity of which this collection only captures a little. There is no doubt that the studies in visual cognition will help us understand how we wish to navigate the ever-complicated world full of objects we have created, both virtual and real. Much of our conscious moments are now spent on a screen that has numbers, digits, pictures and all sorts of visual objects. Both our economic and pleasurable activities depend on how we find objects, project meanings onto them and integrate them into our consciousness. Therefore the theoretical and practical implications of such studies are enormous. The chapters show the power of simple experiments on computers that could help understand how complicated yet flawless human cognition is.

1 Outline of the book

One of the frustrating aspects of attention research is the lack of a unifying model or a framework that encompasses all the different varieties of attention. The result, sometimes, is that different researchers talk about the same thing in a different language. In Chapter 2, Raymond Klein proposes a taxonomy to bring the various shades of attention under a single framework. This three-dimensional model uses Posner's tripartite taxonomy involving alerting, orienting and executive control as the base and builds on this by adding the two modes of attentional control (exogenous, endogenous) and the three domains over which attention operates (time, space and task). The chapter also provides an excellent historical overview of the developments in attention from the era of behaviorism through Hebbian learning to modern-day cognitive-neuroscientific approaches. It serves as a succinct introduction to the different aspects of attention to a reader beginning to get interested in the topic and also provides a coherent framework for experienced researchers to contextualize their research questions.

Understanding the factors that decide what we pay attention to has been one of the most important questions in attention research so far. The traditional view was that our attention is driven either by our goals (e.g., reading a book) or by salient information in the environment (e.g., a loud noise on the street). In Chapter 3, Kim and Anderson first present a brief overview of this dichotomy followed by the accumulated evidence for a third important factor: selection history. Apart from our goals and salience, our recent experiences with a particular stimulus can also determine what we pay attention to. For instance, if you wear a watch every day, you will most likely look at your wrist to know the time even on a day you are not wearing a watch. Experience-driven selection of objects or locations can be of various types. This chapter focuses on key issues such as reward and punishment history. The authors review important studies that have provided evidence for selection-history-driven attentional selection, and importantly, how it has been established to be the third form of attention control, independent of goals and salience. This chapter is an excellent primer for anyone who wants to dive deep into selection history.

Priority map is the most promising model that accounts for the different factors that influence attentional selection. Chapter 4, by Lamy and colleagues, details the concept of a priority map as a psychological framework and also the regions of the brain that are associated with it. This chapter is a nice progression from Chapter 3 because while the last chapter describes the three main sources of attention selection, this chapter examines whether there is a hierarchy among these factors within the priority map. More importantly, the chapter reviews the shortcomings of the traditional understanding of priority maps. They specifically challenge the traditional explanations of spatial cueing effects as seen in the Posner cueing paradigm and offer recent evidence that doesn't neatly fit into existing accounts. The authors end by proposing a new model that attempts to address some of these limitations.

Chapter 5 follows the theme of exploring the factors driving attentional selection and additionally brings in the issue of consciousness. There has been a lively and long-running debate concerning the role of consciousness in attention (and vice versa). In this chapter, Mohite and colleagues take the specific example of distractor avoidance in visual search and examine whether there is enough evidence to claim that human participants can suppress distractors even without being aware of them. The authors focus on two lines of research: visual statistical learning in visual search studies and unconscious cueing in spatial orienting studies to find supporting evidence for this claim. This topic has far-reaching consequences on the role of consciousness in human cognition and the extent to which our ability to regulate our thoughts and actions requires conscious awareness.

Although cognitive psychologists have tried to carve up the various cognitive functions into neatly defined categories such as attention, memory and emotion, among others, it is a well-known fact that these categories often overlap with each other. Chapter 6 demonstrates one such overlap between attention, memory and eye movements. McAteer and colleagues examine the role of eye movements in the encoding, maintenance and retrieval stages of visuospatial short-term memory. Considering the tight link between attention and eye movements, it is critical to understand the role of the oculomotor system in other cognitive functions such as memory if we are to achieve an integrative and holistic understanding of the human mind.

The chapters outlined above describe some of the most interesting advances made in the discipline over the last two decades. While this is worthy of celebration, this sub-field is not without its problems. Several debates have raged on for decades with no clear resolution in sight. Although the larger problems within psychological research such as the replication crisis and lack of concern for cultural and individual variation have not yet plagued attention research, it is probably a matter of time before they do. In Chapter 7, Bernhard Hommel outlines the flaws in current theorizing within psychology and provides clear directions to address them. Many of the points mentioned apply to attention research specifically, but also more generally to human cognition. It is a wider call for action for researchers working across different areas of cognitive psychology. The chapter intentionally has a broad scope to be useful to researchers from different sub-fields as large-scale changes are possible only if a majority of people adopt them. The chapter, and thus the book, ends on a hopeful note on the way forward in the study of the human mind.

One of the advantages of an edited volume on diverse topics is that the chapters can be read in any order. Although the chapters are all related in content to one another, each chapter can be viewed as self-contained. Readers can choose any chapter that most closely matches their interest without having read the previous chapters. Each chapter begins by giving a detailed theoretical background to the issues to be discussed which will hopefully help the reader to appreciate the more complex issues that are discussed later in the chapter. Each chapter ends with suggestions for future research. This is not an exhaustive list of potential research questions but is instead intended to spark ideas and serve as a starting point for future investigations.

We thank all the participants and speakers of the International Conference on Recent Advances in Attention and Cognition for their active participation. The conference was organized with support from an Erasmus+ capacity-building grant to Ramesh Kumar Mishra. We are grateful for this support. Special thanks to Vaishnavi Mohite, who was the student organizer of the conference and who has also assisted in the preparation of this book. Finally, we are deeply grateful to all the authors who contributed. Without their support, this project would not have come together.

2 Thinking about attention

Successive approximations to a productive taxonomy

Raymond M. Klein

1 Introduction

For our discipline, for understanding the organization (and disorganization) of behaviour and thought by our mind and brain (cf, Hebb, 1949), the concept of attention is of fundamental importance. This is not because, as James (1890) famously said, "everyone knows what attention is"; but rather because everyone's behaviours and thoughts are mediated, in one way or another, by some aspect of attention. "Some aspect of attention" is a deliberately selected phrase. The term attention is used to refer to a variety of cognitive processes that share fundamental properties. Scholars and students are sometimes confused when "attention" is being explored or used to help understand something; consequently Hommel, Chapman, Cisek, Neyedli, Song and Welsh (2019) titled a paper "No One Knows What Attention Is." Such confusion might be understandable when the aforementioned variety of *attentions* is a hodgepodge of processes that do not appear to be related. I believe that such confusion can be ameliorated, if not avoided, by a thoughtful organization or taxonomy of the kinds of processes that are subsumed by the term *attention*. Moreover, such a taxonomy, even if not universally endorsed, can be a fruitful stimulus for research.

This chapter begins with a brief history to set the stage for what follows. The history is brief because it is well-known and well-covered by other authors. But it is necessary because the kind of thinking I am doing to construct this chapter has been (benignly) neglected by scholars of attention (though not by scholars in general), despite the important roles that attention contributes to it. This history sets the stage for a description of Posner's tripartite taxonomy of attention and the Attention Network Test, which were developed to assess the efficacy of the three networks of attention identified by this taxonomy. In the next two sections revisions to this taxonomy are presented. Previously described in a chapter by Klein and Lawrence (2011), the first revision entails construing attention as the allocation of resources in the domains of time, space and activity (or task), and, importantly, whether the allocation of resources is controlled by our own intentions (endogenously) or not (exogenously). The second revision, recognizes the importance of the arena in which resources are being allocated: is this overt, in the real, external world where the behaviour of the organism under study can

DOI: 10.4324/9781003360896-2

actually be observed; or, is it covert, in a purely mental, internal world—the world of thought and imagination. "What's next" is considered in the final section where the reader is encouraged to think about challenges to and prospects for the revised taxonomy of attention proposed here.

1.1 Brief history

There was interest in attention, discussions of its importance, and empirical investigations of its aspects in the earliest days of experimental psychology. For an early review, the reader is directed to the "Attention" chapter in James (1890, chapter XI). But as we can see from the material assembled by Michael Posner in volume 1 ("History of Attention from Ancient to Modern Times") of his 4-volume compendium *The Psychology of Attention*, human interest in the topic goes back at least 3000 years (see, Posner, 2016). In the early 1900s Wundt's disciple in North America, Titchener, identified attention as the crucible for our discipline (Titchener 1908). A few years later, criticisms made by Watson (1913) in his so-called "behaviorist manifesto" against what he called "subjective psychology" cast mental constructs like thinking and attention into doubt for the first half of the 20th century.

Chinks in the behaviourist armor began to appear in the 1940s with the failure of a simplistic S-R psychology to help explain many human performance accidents during World War II (Lachman, Lachman & Butterfield, 1979). The need for mental constructs was well understood by Kenneth Craik, who, in *The Nature of Explanation*, hypothesized as follows:

> If the organism carries a small scale model of external reality and of its own possible actions within its head, it is possible to try out various alternatives, conclude which is the best of them, react to future situations before they arise, utilize the knowledge of past events in dealing with the present and the future, and in every day to react in a much fuller, safer and more competent manner to the emergencies which face it.
>
> (Craik, 1943)

Similarly, animal learning psychologist, Edward Tolman (1948) inferred that not only human spatial behaviour but also that of rats required the assumption *cognitive maps*. Claude Shannon's mathematical theory of communication, his quantifiable concept of *information* and its transmission through a noisy channel (Shannon 1948) was adopted by psychologists in the 1950s (e.g. Attneave, 1954; Miller, 1956) who were disenchanted with the radical behaviorism of Watson and Skinner.

Coming from a neuroscientific perspective, but with a deep understanding of psychology's historical roots, Hebb's (1949) landmark book, *Organization of Behavior: A Neuropsychological Theory*, played an important role in setting the stage for a revival of cognitivism. That such a revival may have been Hebb's intention is revealed by the recent discovery (Brown, 2020) that the original title of this book was *On Thought and Behavior*. Indeed, in his preface Hebb asserted that "The failure of psychology to handle thought adequately...has been the essential weakness of modern psychological theory" (Hebb, 1949, p. xvi). In the introduction (Klein, 1980) to a book, *The Nature of Thought*, honouring Hebb, it was suggested that

> through his unflagging emphasis on internal mental processes, his cogent demonstration of weaknesses in some key assumptions of the Gestalt and S-R frameworks, and his own cell-assembly proposal, Hebb may be said to have plowed the soil from which the renaissance in cognitive psychology would grow and flourish.
>
> (Klein, 1980, p. 12)

According to several authors, behaviorism was overthrown by a "cognitive revolution" (for one review, see Lachman et al., 1979) whose leaders convincingly illustrated behaviorism's weaknesses (e.g., Chomsky, 1959) and the fruitfulness, one might say necessity, of a cognitive psychology (Bruner, Goodnow & Austin 1956; Neisser, 1967). Consequently, by the middle of the 20th century the influence of radical behaviorism's aversion to mental constructs, which had dominated experimental psychology—at least in North America –began to wane.

Of particular pertinence to this chapter, Hebb (1949) admonished the field: "Everyone knows that attention and set exist so we had better get the skeleton out of the closet and see what can be done with it." And it was not long before the concept of attention was made respectable and exciting (again) by influential theories (e.g., Broadbent, 1958) and creative experimental paradigms (e.g., Posner, 1980; Posner & Boies, 1971; Posner & Snyder, 1975; Treisman & Gelade, 1980; Treisman & Schmidt, 1982).

2 Posner's tripartite taxonomy

Although the varieties of attention-related concepts have been discussed by a variety of scholars (Kahneman, 1973; Mirsky, Anthony, Duncan, Ahearn & Kellam, 1991; Parasuraman & Davies, 1984) it has been the components of attention described in Michael Posner's work that has garnered the greatest interest (for one review, see Raz & Buhle, 2006). The first iteration of Posner's taxonomy came in his 1971 *Psychological Review* paper with Steve Boies entitled the *Components of Attention*. The components, explored with Posner's signature mental chronometry (Posner, 1978), were: alertness, selection and limited capacity. Almost 20 years later, with Steve Petersen, Posner published *The Attention System of the Human Brain* in the *Annual Review of Neuroscience*. In this hugely influential paper a revised and related taxonomy of attention was proposed (Posner & Petersen, 1990), wherein three isolable but cooperating brain networks each mediated a different set of attentional processes: alerting, orienting and executive control (see Table 2.1).

Table 2.1 Components and networks of attention as proposed by Posner and Boies and Posner and Petersen, respectively.

Posner & Boies (1971)	*Posner & Petersen (1990)*
Selection	Orienting
Alertness	Alertness
Limited capacity	Executive control

The scientific advances that characterize Posner's career are punctuated by his creative development of *model tasks* for exploring basic mental operations. No doubt the subsequent development of a simple model task, the Attention Network Test (Fan, McCandliss, Sommer, Raz & Posner, 2002), that could be used to measure the efficacy of these three networks of attention, played a critical role in encouraging the great interest that Posner's tripartite taxonomy of attention has garnered.

2.1 *The Attention Network Test(s)*

As described by Fan et al. (2002), the original Attention Network Test (ANT) is a simple 2-alternative reaction-time task with different cues that precede different targets. A participant experiencing the ANT would be instructed to report, with a corresponding button press, the direction of a central arrow target presented above or below fixation.

There are 4 cue conditions: no cue, a central cue, a double cue and a spatial cue (above or below fixation). Importantly, following a spatial cue, the target array ALWAYS appeared at the location of the cue. The target is flanked by neutral lines or by arrows pointing in the same or opposite direction as the target arrow. Each of the 4 cue conditions is paired with each of the 6 possible target arrays to yield 24 possible combinations and 12 possible conditions (with direction of the arrow being irrelevant to the computation of network scores).

In the first psychometric analysis of the ANT (MacLeod et al., 2010) the raw data from 15 different publications was subjected to a mega-analysis. Among other things, it was discovered that the results from the seminal Fan et al. paper (Figure 2.1a) were robustly replicated when the data from 1129 participants was analyzed (Figure 2.1b).

In line with Posner's affinity for mental chronometry (see Klein, 2003), the ANT yields 3 subtractions, called "network scores" that are designed to assess the networks responsible for alerting, orienting and executive control.

- Alerting is computed by subtracting reaction times to targets following a double cue from RT to targets following no cue. The assumption is that the double cue allows the participant to prepare for the upcoming target; preparation that is not (or is less) possible without any cue.

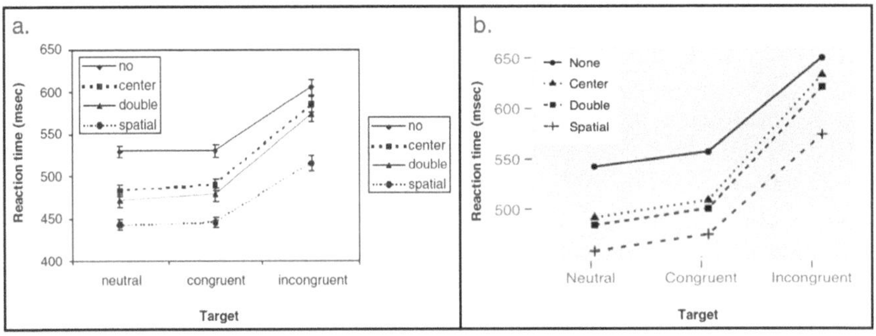

Figure 2.1 Reaction time findings from the Attention Network Test (a) from the seminal study by Fan et al. (2002) and (b) from the psychometric mega-analysis of 15 studies and 1129 participants by MacLeod et al. (2010).

- Orienting is computed by subtracting RT to targets following a spatial cue from RT to targets preceded by a central cue. Here it is assumed that the spatial cue encourages the focussing of visual attention on the location where the target will appear which allows for faster responding than when this location is not signalled in advance.
- Executive control is computed by subtracting RT to targets with congruent flankers from RT to targets with incongruent flankers. The assumption here is that the resolution of response conflict is necessary on incongruent (but not on congruent) trials to avoid responding in the direction of the flankers and that resolution of response conflict is a hallmark of executive control.

From inspection of the results portrayed in Figure 2.1 the reader can see that the aforementioned subtractions would generate robust network scores as well as one striking departure from additivity: Reflecting a decrease in executive control, the executive function score is increased when the participant has been made alert by any cue so long as that cue does not indicate where the target will appear.

Three early interdisciplinary papers from Posner and colleagues demonstrated the remarkable utility of the ANT and the taxonomy upon which it was based and I believe played an important role in the ANT's rapidly growing popularity. Posner et al. (2002) applied the ANT to a psychiatric disorder, borderline personality disorder, discovering a localized attentional deficit in executive control. Fossella et al. (2002) explored the molecular genetics of attention's networks, and using fMRI, Fan, McCandliss, Fossella, Flombaum and Posner (2005) demonstrated that the different conditions used by the ANT to measure alerting, orienting and executive control activated different brain networks.

To be sure, the ANT has some weaknesses. The reliability of some network scores is relatively low. The measures of both orienting and alertness conflate two modes of control (endogenous and exogenous; see section 3 below). And flanker interference may measure something about executive control but, as we have learned from Miyake et al. (2000) and others, it is only a small bit of that construct. But whereas these imperfections are noteworthy, so too are the benefits of the ANT: it is easy to administer, the network scores have been associated with many interesting psychological, psychiatric, psychopharmacological, genetic, neuroscientific findings, and it can be modified to suit new purposes.

Indeed, in the years that followed the early work with the ANT described above, a variety of versions of the ANT were developed for specific purposes. Because these are reviewed in a recent paper entitled, "On the Origins and Evolution of the Attention Network Tests" (Almeida, Faria & Klein, 2021), I will mention just a few of these here. In the "child" ANT (Rueda et al., 2004), to make the task more engaging, the arrows are replaced by colored fish, feedback is added following correct and incorrect responses and a story-line is used: the task is to catch or feed the middle fish by the left or right response button. Aside from the original and child ANTs, the most widely used variant was developed by Callejas and colleagues (Callejas, Lupiáñez, Funes & Tudela, 2005). Their variation, called the ANT-I, or ANT-Interaction, was the original ANT with two important modifications: (1) alertness was generated by an auditory tone; this change permitted orienting and alertness to be manipulated independently and therefore, in principle, to allow researchers to explore their interaction, and (2) the peripheral cues used to explore orienting were made entirely uninformative. This latter change was motivated by a weakness of the ANT that will be revisited in section 3: Because the ANT uses peripheral cues that are 100% informative[1] about the location of the upcoming target, it confounds two modes of control of orienting: exogenous because the cues are in the periphery; and endogenous because of the cues' informativeness about where the target will appear. The ANT-I, in contrast, generates a pure form of exogenous orienting.

Among the many variants, we are particularly excited about our game-like variant, the *AttentionTrip* that we developed anticipating that it would be more engaging than the typical ANTs (Klein, Hassan, Wilson, Ishigami & Mulle, 2017). The need for engagement was encouraged by the possibility that boredom might compromise the value of the computed network scores (e.g., Matthews, Warm, Reinerman, Langheim & Saxby, 2010) and the fact that this problem would be exacerbated in studies that required assessing the networks of attention in multiple sessions (e.g., when testing the effectiveness of treatment for attention problems or a method for improving attention). The participant is presented with one of two narratives involving steering a vehicle and shooting at targets. In one narrative the vehicle is a miniaturized medical ship being driven through a blood vessel and the targets are different viruses; in the other narrative it's a spaceship being driven through a worm-hole. The AttentionTrip generates robust network scores and has been demonstrated to be more engaging than the ANT for both adults (Klein, Vallis & Chisholm, 2019) and children (Arora, McCormick & Klein, 2021). Whereas the original version[2] required a desktop computer and gaming steering-wheel, we have recently portabilized the AttentionTrip and it is now operational on the iPad. With this development the AttentionTrip can now be run without a desktop computer and without the clunky gaming steering wheel (see Klein, McCormick, Almeida, Lawen & Arora, 2024).

2.2 *Attention network test database*

A vast literature has not only paid attention to the ANT and its variants; a rapidly growing number of studies have been conducted using it with an even more striking growth in the number of participants who have been tested. This growth (see Figure 2.2) encouraged the creation of a publicly searchable database in which is stored information about the network scores generated by every publication using any version of the ANT to explore any question (http://attentionnetwork.ca). The database was described in an open-source article (Arora, Lawrence and Klein, 2020) in which two meta-analytic uses were illustrated: ADHD was shown to robustly affect alerting and executive control, but not orienting; and, experiments conducted in China have found smaller executive scores than those conducted in Europe or North America. Since then, the database been used to explore how bilingualism (Arora, Lawrence and Klein, 2020), depression (Sinha, Arora, Srivastava & Klein, 2022), autism (Good, Arora, Townsend, Mash & Klein, 2022) and lifestyle choices (McCormick, 2022) might affect or be associated with the networks of attention.

3 First revision: two modes of control operating in three domains

Ironically, Posner's development of model tasks for exploring visual orienting suggests that an important distinction is missing from his tripartite taxonomy and from the ANT: mode of control. Between 1975 and 1980 Posner developed and described these tasks in presentations at the annual meetings of the Psychonomic Society that culminated in these three seminal publications: Posner, Nissen & Ogden (1978), Posner (1980), and Posner, Snyder & Davidson (1980). One model task elicited a voluntary form of orienting, that Posner (1980) referred to as endogenous; the other elicited a more reflexive form that was referred to as exogenous.

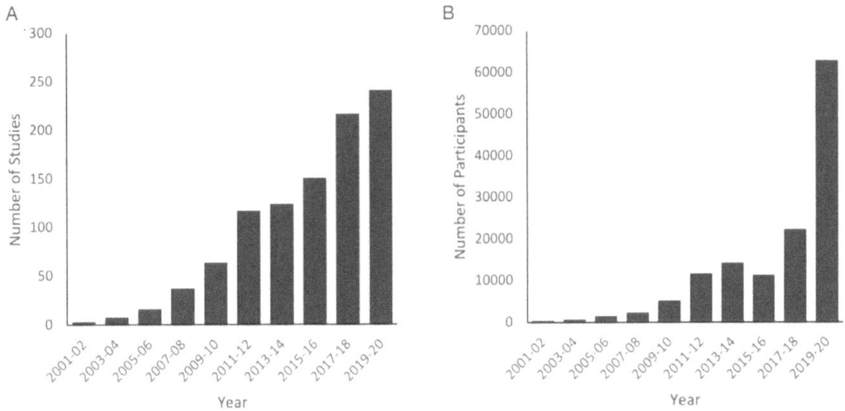

Figure 2.2 (a) Number of studies that used the ANT or a variant of the ANT and (b) number of participants tested in ANT studies.

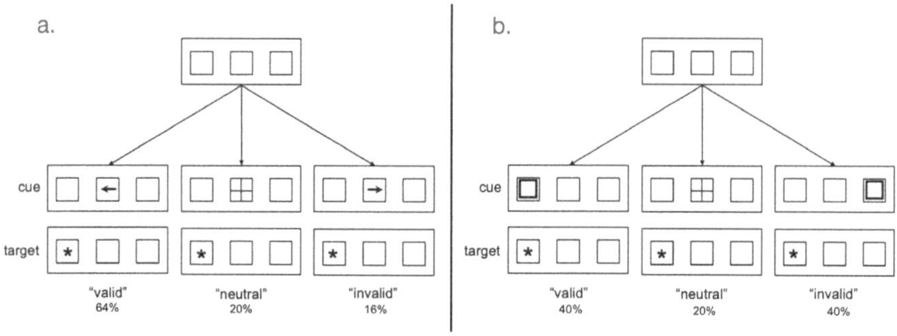

Figure 2.3 Two model tasks for exploring visual orienting: (a) endogenous orienting and (b) exogenous orienting.

In the endogenous version (Figure 2.3a) a stimulus (e.g., arrow or color patch) presented at fixation indicates the likely location of the upcoming target. Importantly such central cues are not presented in locations where the upcoming target might be displayed. In the exogenous version (Figure 2.3b) a peripheral cue is presented and this cue is uninformative about the location of the upcoming target. Importantly, the peripheral cue is presented at locations where the targets might be presented and thus either stimulates the pathway of the upcoming target (as illustrated here for a so-called "valid" trial) or stimulates a pathway distant from where the upcoming target would be presented (on an "invalid" trial). With the proper cue-target timing, the typical pattern of results is obtained: response times are faster for targets presented on valid than on invalid trials, with the neutral condition, often having an intermediate value.

Posner (1993) defined a *model task* by analogy with the notion of a model system in neurobiology: The simplest system that exhibits the target property. In psychological science a model task is the simplest one that allows us to explore the operations of a particular cognitive system. Posner's model tasks for exploring orienting are meant to exemplify pure forms of the kinds of orienting that could be generated in our everyday behaviour. It is important to recognize that in the real-world the purity that these model tasks aim for is rarely achieved (Kingstone, Smilek, Ristic, Kelland Friesen & Eastwood, 2003). The realization that a model task may be lacking in ecological validity does not invalidate its use; Rather, it suggests that more complex and less pure methods may be required to achieve a more complete understanding of the cognitive operations under study.

In the period shortly after the development of these two "Posner cuing tasks" it was generally assumed that one and the same metaphorical "beam" of attention (Posner et al., 1980) was being controlled in two different ways (e.g., see Jonides, 1981): One mode of "transportation" was slow, strategic and voluntary (top-down); the other was fast, automatic, and reflexive (bottom-up); but regardless of the mode of control, the same processing resources were recruited to the cued location. Some researchers still hold this *single beam* view, but research from my lab and later from others strongly suggests otherwise.

The first dissociation was discovered by Briand (Briand, 1984; Briand & Klein, 1987) who combined the aforementioned Posner cuing paradigms with a target identification task that either did (conjunction) or did not (feature) afford the opportunity for illusory conjunctions (Treisman & Schmidt, 1982). He found that when controlled exogenously spatial attention interacted with opportunities for illusory conjunctions (a similar interaction was contemporaneously reported by Prinzmetal, Presti & Posner, 1986) while the pattern was additive when attention was controlled endogenously. Briand and Klein (1987) therefore concluded that when controlled exogenously Posner's beam is the same as Triesman's glue; but when controlled endogenously it is not. This empirical dissociation was later replicated by Briand (1998) in a study designed to address some critical comments of Tsal (1989) and Experiment 3 of Briand (1998; endogenous cuing) was recently replicated by Drake and Klein (2022). When the task relevant stimuli are spread around the display so that they are simultaneously presented at both cued and uncued locations[3] exceptions to Briand's patterns have been reported (Henderickx, Maetens & Soetens, 2010, experiments 1 and 3; Kawahara & Miyatani, 2001). Importantly, as far as I know, so long as all the task-relevant stimuli are presented at *either* the cued or uncued locations this dissociation has been replicated (e.g., see Henderickx et al., 2010, experiment 2).

Other research from the Klein lab generated the opposite pattern of additivity and interaction when the two forms of control of visual orienting were combined with non-spatial expectancies (Klein, 1994). Participants made a size change discrimination for targets presented at a cued as compared to an uncued location. Our non-spatial expectancy was that one change (large or small) and the corresponding response was much more likely than the other one. As expected, responses to more likely targets were faster than to unlikely ones. Importantly, endogenously controlled spatial orienting interacted with this effect, whereas an additive pattern was observed with exogenous control. This dissociation between exogenous and endogenous orienting when combined with a form expectancy is replicated and extended by Kingstone (1993). In contrast to Klein (1994), there was no response expectancy, and both form and location were cued on a trial-by-trial basis. As described in Klein:

> Form was cued endogenously with an SOA of 1200 ms; location was cued exogenously or endogenously at two shorter SOAs. When endogenous control of spatial orienting was combined with endogenous control of a form/object expectancy, there was a clear interaction. However, when a purely exogenous location cue was used (uninformative abrupt peripheral luminance change), or both were combined (abrupt peripheral luminance change with meaning) using an SOA too short to allow the subject to generate an endogenous expectancy, the shape expectancy was additive with spatial orienting.
>
> (Klein, 1994, p. 176)

From this double dissociation (see the top two rows of Table 2.2) it was inferred that there must be two metaphorical beams of attention. Furthermore, as

Table 2.2 Dissociations between exogenous and endogenous control of attention in space.

Effect	*Endogenous control*	*Exogenous control*
Interacts with illusory conjunctions?	No	Yes
Interacts with non-spatial expectancies?	Yes	No
Extra cost for crossing a meridian	Yes	No
Effect on spatial Stroop?	Increases	Decreases
Disengage deficit with parietal damage?	Small	Large
Does it generate illusory line motion?	No	Yes
Generates inhibition of return?	No	Yes

Sources: adapted from Klein and Lawrence (2012)

illustrated in Table 2.2, when you look for them, dissociations are seen outside the Klein laboratory (for reviews, see Klein, 2009 and Klein & Lawrence, 2011) and in many other contexts.[4] Thus, if we construe "orienting" as the allocation of resources in space, we must conclude that qualitatively different resources are allocated when the control of orienting is exogenous versus endogenous. Importantly, as noted in section 2.1, because the ANT uses peripheral cues that are informative about the location of the upcoming target, it conflates these two modes of control of orienting.

The distinction between endogenous and exogenous control applies equally to what Posner's taxonomy refers to as alertness (Lawrence & Klein, 2013; see also Coull, Frith, Büchel & Nobre, 2000), which we describe as the allocation of resources in time (Klein & Lawrence, 2011). As noted by Lawrence and Klein (2013) most studies of alertness that have varied the foreperiod between a warning signal and a target, have confounded these two sources of control (much as the original ANT confounded them for orienting). The signal typically entails a change in intensity and targets, even when catch trials or non-aging foreperiods are used, are always preceded by and therefore contingently related to these signals. The change in intensity allows for the possibility of a reflexive form of temporal attention: a temporary change in arousal. The contingency allows for a volitional form of temporal attention: preparation.

In a two-choice visual discrimination task, Lawrence and Klein (2013) used a change in white noise from diotic to dichotic as a signal. Importantly, this easily detectable change was accompanied or not by an increase in intensity. The intense signals were assumed to generate some degree of arousal that the iso-intense signals would not generate. A manipulation of contingency was factorially combined with these two signal types: In the contingent condition (in a series of blocks, each with a different foreperiod) the signal, whether intense or iso-intense, was predictably followed by the target. In the non-contingent condition, modelled after Rescorla's *truly random control condition* (Rescorla, 1967) the signals and targets were generated independently. This combination of novel methods allowed Lawrence and Klein to successfully dissociate endogenous from exogenous temporal attention. And the independence of these two modes of control of attention in time was later confirmed by McCormick, Redden, Lawrence and Klein (2018).

Building on the important distinction just illustrated, we presented a revised taxonomy of attention, entitled "The Modes and Domains of Attention" in the 2nd edition of Posner's edited volume *The Cognitive Neuroscience of Attention*:

> All living things are information-processing systems, each collecting information about the environment and internal states, then using this information to direct behavior toward the immediate and ultimate goals of the system. Some systems manifest rudimentary processing, whereby signals elicit reflexive responses in a manner that has been tuned by natural selection. Other systems additionally permit more complex processing, including storage and comparison to memory, whereby an individual's history of experienced contingencies can motivate more nuanced behavior. However, information processing in both biological and artificial systems is an energy costly undertaking, and thus efficient systems are those that achieve preferential allocation of processing resources to signals and signal domains that pertain most strongly to the goals of the system. We operationalize attention as this differential allocation of information processing resources, whereby allocation can be achieved by multiple modes and within multiple domains.
>
> (Klein & Lawrence, 2012, p. 11)

In the original version of this revised taxonomy, the domains we proposed were space, time, modality and task (or activity). In subsequent descriptions, modality was incorporated into the domain of space. When it is recognized that there are two modes of control of resource allocation, exogenous and endogenous the revised taxonomy becomes a 2×3 matrix as illustrated in Table 2.3 where its relation to Posner's tripartite taxonomy can be visualized.

Table 2.3 Revised taxonomy proposed by Klein and Lawrence (2011) and its relation to the taxonomy from Posner and Petersen (1990) upon which the original ANT is based.

Original taxonomy	*Revised taxonomy*		
		Mode of control	
Network	Domain	Exogenous (bottom-up)	Endogenous (top-down)
Orienting	Space	Capture	Expectancy
Alertness	Time	Alertness	Arousal
Executive control	Activity (or task)	Instinct/habit	Choice

Following this revised taxonomy six scores are needed to fully characterize attention. Some possible labels for the six combinations of mode of control and domain of operation might be, for exogenous versus endogenous control in the three domains: alertness versus preparation, capture versus expectancy and instinct/habit versus choice, for the domains of time, space and task/activity.

3.1 The CAST

Building on this taxonomic "improvement," Mike Lawrence (2018) developed the Combined Attention Systems Test (CAST), which generates six separate measures of attentional allocation in the domains of space, time and task under exogenous and endogenous control. There are two "sub-tests." Each incorporates measures of both modes of control in the domain of task or activity. The control of attention in space and time is exogenous in one sub-test and endogenous in the other. Lawrence demonstrated the psychometric viability of this test in his 2018 dissertation (Lawrence, 2018; see also Lawrence, Johnson, Arora & Klein, 2022): When testing young adults all six RT-based network scores were significantly different from zero and reasonably reliable. Similar results were obtained with children when the CAST was successfully used in a research project exploring the effect upon attention from exposure to nature (Johnson et al., 2019).

4 Second revision: arena of operation

Of course, we all know that orienting can be overt (as when we move our eyes to the location where important information might be encoded) or covert (as when our attention is shifted in the absence of an observable behaviour in the real world). For this reason, variants of Figure 2.4, which is based on Posner (1980), have been used to illustrate what I reckon to be four kinds of orienting.

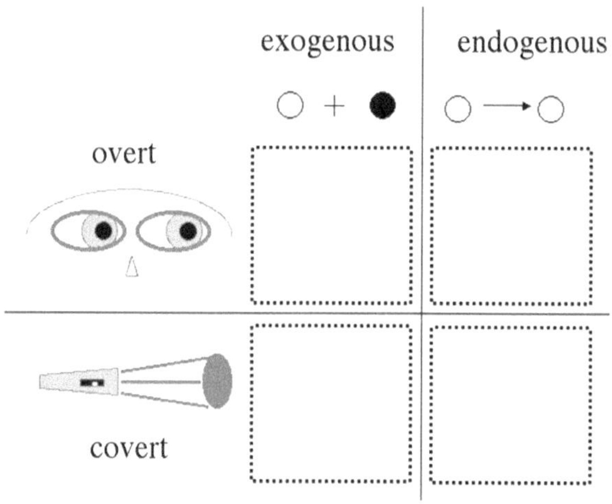

Figure 2.4 A 2×2 matrix is used to illustrate the distinction between overt and covert orienting and their control by exogenous and endogenous mechanisms.
Source: reproduced from Klein (2005)

Thus, there is a further distinction that I believe our revised taxonomy requires. I think it is very important—particularly for understanding the direction of our thinking and our imaginative activities. Consider the 2×3 taxonomy presented in section 3 with its two modes of control and three domains. Imagine, if you will, (before you look at Figure 2.5) the 2×2 matrix from Figure 2.4, with its distinctions between endogenous and exogenous control of overt and covert orienting, incorporated into the top layer (*domain* of *space*) and penetrating downward through the entire taxonomy.

This final distinction (overt/covert) concerns whether the arena in which resources are being recruited or allocated is happening in the real, external world where the behavior of the organism under study can actually be observed or, if it is taking place in a purely mental, internal world—the world of thought and imagination. This covert, internal arena is precisely the mental world that behaviorism had cast aside. Craik (1943) had imagined the importance of our internalized representational capacity for safety. Humphrey (1984) imagined its importance for the evolution of consciousness. After noting the importance of humans as social beings, for whom predicting (Humphrey doesn't say it, but also controlling) the behavior of others would convey great selective advantages, he puts forward this essential thesis:

> Nature's solution to the problem of doing psychology has been to give every member of the human species both the power and inclination to use a privileged picture his own self as a model for what it is like to be another person.
>
> (Humphrey, 1984, p. 6)

Not only can we "think" but we understand that other people we are interacting with are thinking too.

In contrast to our observable actions in the external world, the psychological scientist must infer the invisible mental operations through carefully designed

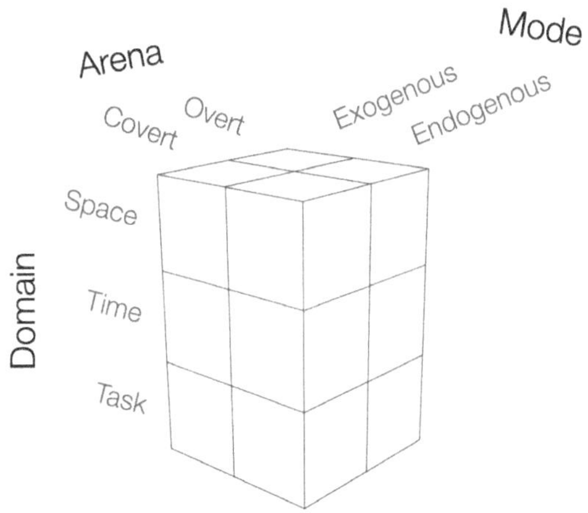

Figure 2.5 Revised taxonomy of attention.

experiments. Modern and ever-improving neuroimaging methods have been and will continue to be, a great aid in this endeavour, because they allow us to see the activity in the brain that is associated with the hypothesized mental activity.

Of course, the idea that thinking is important in psychological theory is not a new one. Indeed, the cognitive revolution turned an excited and fruitful eye upon this important topic. In a 1979 symposium entitled *Consciousness in Contemporary Psychology* (Puccetti & Klein, 1980), Posner was one of the speakers and his presentation was entitled: "Orienting to Visual and Semantic Space: Some Common Features of Conscious Processing." A few years later, Posner, Rafal, Choate and Vaughan (1985) revisited this theme and ended a paper about inhibition of return with the speculative hope that "our new results also provide some connections between the scanning process involved in orienting attention to visual locations and those related to orienting in memory" (p. 226). The distinction between externally and internally directed attention (while somewhat different from the distinction I have drawn) is also not new (Chun, Golomb & Turk-Browne, 2011). But the incorporation of this distinction into the kind of full taxonomy of attention that I have presented here is new. I hope it will be useful and fruitful.

5 What's next?

The subtitle of this chapter ("Successive approximations to a productive taxonomy") draws inspiration from George Sperling's "Successive Approximations to a Model for Short Term Memory" (Sperling, 1967). Two things struck me about this paper. First it built inventively upon Sperling's (1960) ground-breaking discovery of what Neisser (1967) would later popularize as "iconic memory"; second, it implicitly acknowledged that our current conceptualizations are almost always imperfect and improvable. This universal truth suggests that further thinking is almost always needed. Indeed, stimulating thought is a principal objective of this chapter. It is hoped that the ideas herein will encourage attention researchers to think about how the rich conceptual toolbox they have developed to understand (particularly visual) attention might be applied to illuminate thinking. And conversely, that researchers interested in thinking will find the distinctions implied by the revised taxonomy presented here both interesting and fruitful.

5.1 Challenges

As implied by "successive approximations," the taxonomy presented in Figure 2.5 is an improvable approximation. To each reader of this chapter different puzzles and possible solutions may come to mind. In this section, I will point to a few challenges. There is no effort to be exhaustive here; rather these are meant to serve as examples to stimulate further thinking.

One challenge comes from work on visual attention. We not only have the ability to attend to locations in space, but also to non-spatial features that may characterize objects in our visual environment, such as colour, motion and orientation. And the power of this form of visual attention to exclude from awareness objects that do not match what we are looking for is impressive (e. g., see Simons & Chabris, 1999). This activates the idea that in the proposed taxonomy perhaps "orienting," the "allocation of resources in space," might be recast as the "allocation of resources to an input pathway." A related issue goes back (at least) to the Gestalt vs Structuralist debate whether features or objects are primary in perception. In the area of visual attention this debate was brought into focus by Duncan's (1984) seminal demonstration.

Another challenge is related to the important distinction between exogenous and endogenous modes of control. When described as a dichotomy (Awh, Belopolsky & Theeuwes, 2012) such a scheme may be untoward because there are many examples that do not fit neatly into one or the other category. In a "news from the field" article I commented upon a debate that ensued following a session on "attention capture" at the 2016 meeting of the Psychonomic Society. Whereas the debate and this commentary was about orienting the message applies to the endogenous/exogenous distinction regardless of the domain in which control is operating:

> At the end of the first "attention capture" session a debate ensued concerning how we distinguish between and label the different ways attention might be controlled. There is pretty good agreement that attention can be controlled bottom-up primarily by information in the incoming stimulus and topdown primarily by our momentary goals. Some, following Posner (1980), use the terms exogenous and endogenous when referring to this distinction which is loosely associated with reflexive and voluntary control (Jonides, 1981). The debate was about the usefulness of this distinction in the face of forms of control (e.g., selection history; gaze cuing; learning; phobias) that do not neatly fall into one type or the other. Because a dichotomy divides the world of possibilities into two pure categories, it may be a failed dichotomy (Awh et al., 2012). But it is not a failed distinction. A distinction doesn't lose its value simply because some tokens don't fall neatly into one or the other type. One attitude toward these ambiguous forms is to accept their lack of "purity" and to explore them, determining the conditions for eliciting each form and the nature of each form's effects on performance (e.g., Klein, 2009).
>
> (Klein, 2017, pp. 1–2)

Perhaps the most exciting challenge will be to connect the revised taxonomy to the underlying neuroscience. Beginning with the "where" question, we can ask: Where in the brain are the representations and computations that mediate the different forms of attention identified in the revised taxonomy located? The primary sources of evidence on this question have been from neuropsychology and neuroimaging. The evidence accumulated and summarized by Posner and colleagues (Fan et al., 2005; Petersen & Posner, 2012; Posner & Petersen, 1990; Posner & Raichle, 1994) for the tripartite taxonomy provides a starting point.

Considerable work has been done on the distinction between endogenous and exogenous modes of control (introduced in section 3) particularly in the covert arena for the domain of space. This was reviewed by Chica, Bartolomeo and Lupiáñez (2013) who concluded that endogenous and exogenous spatial attention are implemented by overlapping, but partially segregated networks. For the more segregated systems, they identified a dorsal fronto-parietal network as involved in endogenous control and the right temporo-parietal junction as involved in exogenous control. Overlapping and segregated networks have also been identified for the endogenous versus exogenous control of overt attention in space (Mort et al., 2003), and for the endogenous/exogenous distinction in the domain of time (Coull, Frith, Büchel & Nobre, 2000). Consider next, the allocation of attention in the domain of actions and the distinction (introduced in section 4.0) between the overt and covert arenas. The execution of actions would be in the overt arena of the real world while planning or imagining the same actions would be in the covert arena, the internal world of thought or imagination. Neuroimaging data (for a review, see Hardwick, Caspers, Eichoff & Swinnen, 2018) demonstrates that while there is considerable overlap in the brain regions activated by executing and imagining the same actions, there is also considerable non-overlap. The distinctions proposed in the revised taxonomy of Figure 2.5 are buttressed by these examples of non-overlapping neural networks that correspond to them.

5.2 *Prospects*

In *The Evolution of the Brain and Intelligence*, Jerison (1973) hypothesized that when a species's brain was big relative to its body size, the excess neural machinery was available to increase intelligence. Humans, according to Jerison, have the highest ratio of brain to body size, and this excess has allowed us to be flexible, to self-regulate, communicate, represent, predict and problem solve. To be sure, many species can do some of these things; and some species can do some of them very well. But on our planet, only humans have developed writing systems, which we have used to write papers and deliver talks like this one (not to mention foment revolutions, justify genocide and create enduring cultures), figured out how to leave the planet and might even be in the process of destroying it.

After describing six views of embodied cognition, Wilson draws a conclusion that connects to Jerison's hypothesis and fits well with my own views (Klein 2020):

> Off-line aspects of embodied cognition, in contrast, include any cognitive activities in which sensory and motor resources are brought to bear on mental tasks whose referents are distant in time and space or are altogether imaginary. These include symbolic off-loading, where external resources are used to assist in the mental representation and manipulation of things that are not present, as well as purely internal uses of sensorimotor representations, in the form of mental simulations. In these cases, rather than the mind operating to serve the body, we find the body (or its control

> systems) serving the mind. This takeover by the mind, and the concomitant ability to mentally represent what is distant in time or space, may have been one of the driving forces behind the runaway train of human intelligence that separated us from other hominids.
>
> (Wilson, 2002, p. 635)

In *Research on Attention Networks as a Model for the Integration of Psychological Science*, Posner and Rothbart (2007) essentially conclude that Titchener was correct to put the concept of attention at center stage. And they praise Hebb for providing:

> a basis for viewing brain activity in terms of networks that could compute the various functions underlying human thoughts and feelings. He also attempted to treat all the issues that would normally be included in elementary psychology textbooks in terms of this common framework. With the addition of new methods, we believe that the task of integrating all aspects of scientific psychology in a common framework is even more feasible than when Hebb undertook it.
>
> (Posner & Rothbart, 2007, pp. 18–19)

Time will tell if the revised taxonomy of attention I have presented here will affect the thinking of those of you who read this chapter and will stimulate the kind of research that Posner and Rothbart believed could help integrate our discipline.

Notes

1 The ANT-R (Fan et al., 2009) uses cues that are 80% informative. In contrast o the original ANT (with its 100% valid cues), this provides an invalid condition as a baseline against which to assess the orienting effect generated by the cues. Nevertheless, because these cues are in the periphery, endogenous and exogenous control remain conflated when using the ANT-R.
2 See www.youtube.com/watch?v=T5CuMRKTUHw.
3 It is noteworthy that Briand's question "Is Posner's beam the same as Treisman's glue?" was not about search, per se, but rather about the interaction between attentional orienting and the opportunity for illusory conjunctions. For this reason Briand presented arrays of two items that either contained the target or when it didn't it contained features that might or might not afford an illusory impression (conjunction) that the target was present. Introducing a search task across the entire display adds a level of complexity that may produce interesting effects that do not directly address Briand's question.
4 For one example, not covered in Table 2.2, see Lu and Dosher (2000).

Acknowledgements

This chapter, with minor changes, is reproduced from: Klein, R. M. (2022) Thinking about attention: Successive approximations to a productive taxonomy. *Cognition*, 225, 105137 with permission from the publisher.

This chapter is dedicated to Michael Posner, from whom, as the reader will see, I learned everything I needed to know to write it. The revised taxonomy described here was first presented (Klein & Lawrence, 2011) at an international symposium entitled: "On the future of attention research and practice: Defining, measuring and repairing the networks of attention." A recently delivered, albeit revised and updated, reprisal of that presentation (Klein, 2021), provided the impetus to put the ideas into writing in the hope that they might be published and thereby reach a wider audience. I am indebted to the Natural Sciences and Research Council of Canada which has supported my basic research continuously since 1975. The Nova Scotia Health Research Foundation and Dalhousie University's Brain Repair Centre provided funds for specific projects described herein.

References

Almeida, R., Faria, A. & Klein, R. M. (2021). On the origins and evolution of the Attention Network Tests. *Neuroscience and Biobehavioral Reviews*, 126, 560–572.

Arora, S., McCormick, C. R. & Klein, R. M. (2021). Comparing youth engagement on the AttentionTrip to the Child Attention Network Test. *International Journal of Human–Computer Interaction*, 37 (9), 828–834.

Arora, S., Lawrence, M. A. & Klein, R. M. (2020) The Attention Network Test database and some examples of its application, *Frontiers in Psychology*, 11:388. doi:10.3389/fpsyg.2020.00388.

Attneave, F. (1954). Some informational aspects of visual perception. *Psychological Review*, 61 (3), 183–193.

Awh, E., Belopolsky, A. V. & Theeuwes, J. (2012). Top-down versus bottom-up attentional control: A failed theoretical dichotomy. *Trends in Cognitive Sciences*, 16 (8), 437–443.

Briand, K. (1984). Illusory conjunctions & spatial orientation of attention. An Investigation of Treisman's' model. Master's thesis, Dalhousie University.

Briand, K. A. (1998). Feature integration and spatial attention: More evidence of a dissociation between endogenous and exogenous orienting. *Journal of Experimental Psychology: Human Perception and Performance*, 24, 1243–1256.

Briand, K. & Klein, R. M. (1987). Is Posner's beam the same as Treisman's glue?: On the relationship between visual orienting and feature integration theory. *Journal of Experimental Psychology: Human Perception and Performance*, 13, 228–247.

Broadbent, D.E. (1958) *Perception and communication*. Pergamon.

Brown, R. E. (2020). Donald O. Hebb and the organization of behavior: 17 years in the writing. *Molecular Brain*, 13 (1), 1–28.

Bruner. J. S., Goodnow, J. J. & Austin, G. (1956) *A study of thinking*. Wiley.

Callejas, A., Lupiáñez, J., Funes, M. J. & Tudela, P. (2005). Modulations among the alerting, orienting and executive control networks. *Experimental Brain Research*, 167 (1), 27–37.

Callejas, A., Lupiáñez, J. & Tudela, P. (2004). The three attentional networks: On their independence and interactions. *Brain and Cognition*, 54 (3), 225–227.

Chica, A. B., Bartolomeo, P. & Lupiáñez, J. (2013). Two cognitive and neural systems for endogenous and exogenous spatial attention. *Behavioural Brain Research*, 237, 107–123.

Chomsky, N. (1959) Review of Verbal Behavior. By B. F. Skinner. *Language*, 35, 26–58.

Chun, M. M., Golomb, J. D. & Turk-Browne, N. B. (2011). A taxonomy of external and internal attention. *Annual Review of Psychology*, 62, 73–101.

Coull, J. T., Frith, C. D., Büchel, C. & Nobre, A. C. (2000). Orienting attention in time: behavioural and neuroanatomical distinction between exogenous and endogenous shifts. *Neuropsychologia*, 38 (6), 808–819.

Craik, K. J. W. (1943) *The nature of explanation.* Cambridge University Press.

Drake, R. & Klein, R. M. (2022) Posner's endogenous beam is (still) not Treisman's glue. Manuscript submitted for publication.

Duncan. J. (1984). Selective attention and the organisation of visual information. *Journal of Experimental Psychology: General*, 113, 501–517.

Fan, J., Gu, X., Guise, K. G., Liu, X., Fossella, J., Wang, H. & Posner, M. I. (2009). Testing the behavioral interaction and integration of attentional networks. *Brain and Cognition*, 70 (2), 209–220.

Fan, J., McCandliss, B. D., Fossella, J., Flombaum, J. I. & Posner, M. I. (2005). The activation of attentional networks. *Neuroimage*, 26 (2), 471–479.

Fan, J., McCandliss, B. D., Sommer, T., Raz, A. & Posner, M. I. (2002). Testing the efficiency and independence of attentional networks. *Journal of Cognitive Neuroscience*, 14 (3), 340–347.

Fan, J., Wu, Y., Fossella, J. A. & Posner, M. I. (2001). Assessing the heritability of attentional networks. *BMC Neuroscience*, 2 (1), 14.

Fossella, J., Sommer, T., Fan, J., Wu, Y., Swanson, J. M., Pfaff, D. W. & Posner, M. I. (2002). Assessing the molecular genetics of attention networks. *BMC Neuroscience*, 3 (1), 1–11.

Funes, M. J., Lupiáñez, J. & Milliken B. (2007). Separate mechanisms recruited by exogenous and endogenous spatial cues: Evidence from a spatial Stroop paradigm. *Journal of Experimental Psychology: Human Perception and Performance*, 33, 348–362.

Good, S., Arora, S., Townsend, J., Mash, L. & Klein, R. M. (2022). Examining autism spectrum disorder using the Attention Network Test: A meta-analysis. Unpublished manuscript.

Hardwick, R. M., Caspers, S., Eichoff, S. B. & Swinnen, S. P. (2018). Neural correlates of action: Comparing meta-analyses of imagery, observation, and execution. *Neuroscience & Biobehavioral Reviews*, 94, 31–44.

Hebb, D. O. (1949). *The organization of behaviour: A neuropsychological theory.* Wiley.

Henderickx, D., Maetens, K. & Soetens, E. (2010). Feature integration and spatial attention: common processes for endogenous and exogenous orienting. *Psychological Research*, 74 (3), 239–254.

Hommel, B., Chapman, C. S., Cisek, P., Neyedli, H. F., Song, J. H. & Welsh, T. N. (2019). No one knows what attention is. *Attention, Perception & Psychophysics*, 81 (7), 2288–2303.

Humphrey, N. (1984) *Consciousness regained: Chapters in the development of mind.* Oxford University Press.

James, W. (1890). *The principles of psychology.* Henry Holt & Co.

Jerison, H. J. (1973). *The evolution of the brain and intelligence.* Academic Press.

Johnson, S.A., Snow, S., Lawrence, M.A., Rainham, D.G.C. (2019). Quasi-randomized trial of contact with nature and effects on attention in children. *Frontiers in Psychology*, 10, 2652. doi:10.17605/OSF.IO/52AQT.

Jonides, J. (1981). Voluntary versus automatic control over the mind's eye's movement. In J. B. Long & A. D. Baddeley (Eds.), *Attention & Performance IX* (pp. 187–203). Erlbaum.

Kahneman, D. (1973). *Attention and effort.* Prentice-Hall.

Kawahara, J. I. & Miyatani, M. (2001). The effect of informative and uninformative cueing of attention on feature integration. *The Journal of General Psychology*, 128 (1), 57–75.

Kingstone, A. (1993). Endogenous and exogenous orienting during the maintenance of a form expectancy. Unpublished manuscript.

Kingstone, A., Smilek, D., Ristic, J., Kelland Friesen, C. & Eastwood, J. D. (2003). Attention, researchers! It is time to take a look at the real world. *Current Directions in Psychological Science*, 12 (5), 176–180.

Klein, R. M. (1980). D.O. Hebb: An appreciation. In P. Jusczyk & R. M. Klein (Eds.), *On the nature of thought: Essays in honour of D.O. Hebb* (pp. 1–18). Erlbaum Associates.

Klein, R. M. (1994). Perceptual-motor expectancies interact with covert visual orienting under conditions of endogenous but not exogenous control. *Canadian Journal of Experimental Psychology/Revue canadienne de psychologie expérimentale*, 48(2), 167.

Klein, R. M. (2003). Chronometric explorations of disordered minds. *Trends in Cognitive Sciences*, 7 (5), 190–192.

Klein, R. M. (2005). On the role of endogenous orienting in the inhibitory aftermath of exogenous orienting. In U. Mayr, E. Awh & S. Keele (Eds.), *Developing individuality in the human brain: A tribute to Michael I. Posner* (pp. 45–64). APA Books.

Klein, R. M. (2009) On the control of attention. *Canadian Journal of Experimental Psychology*, 63, 240–252.

Klein, R. M. (2017) News from the field: Psychonomics in Boston: A debate about types of orienting, *Attention Perception & Psychophysics*, 79, p. 1–2.

Klein, R. M. (2020). Is covert spatial orienting embodied or disembodied cognition? A historical review. *Quarterly Journal of Experimental Psychology*, 73 (1), 20–28.

Klein, R. M. (2021). *Pursuing a productive taxonomy of attention.* Invited presentation at the International Conference on Recent Advancements in Attention and Cognition, Hyderabad, April.

Klein, R. M., Hassan, T., Wilson, G., Ishigami, Y. & Mulle, J. (2017) The Attention-Trip: A game-like tool for measuring the networks of attention. *Journal of Neuroscience Methods*, 289, 99–109.

Klein, R. M. & Lawrence, M. A. (2011) *The modes and domains of attention. In M. I. Posner (Ed.) Cognitive Neuroscience of Attention* (2nd Ed.). Guilford Press, p. 11–28.

Klein, R. M. & Lawrence, M. A. (2012, May) *Pursuing a productive taxonomy of attention.* Presented at On the future of attention research and practice: Defining, measuring and repairing the networks of attention: An international Symposium, Halifax, Canada.

Klein, R. M., McCormick, C. R., Almeida, R. de S., Lawen, Z., & Arora, S. (2024). Introducing the portable AttentionTrip: An engaging tool for measuring the networks of attention. *Journal of Neuroscience Methods*, 409, 110194.

Klein, R. M., Vallis, E. H. & Chisholm, J. (2019) A Comparison of Engagement between the Attention Network Test and a Game-like version, called the AttentionTrip. *International Journal of Human-Computer Interaction*, 35:19, 1813–1819.

Lachman, R., Lachman, J. L. & Butterfield, E. C. (1979) *Cognitive psychology and information processing: An introduction.* Lawrence Erlbaum Associates.

Lawrence, M. (2018). Developing and validating a combined attention systems test. Dissertation, Dalhousie University.

Lawrence, M. A., Johnson, S. A., Arora, S. & Klein, R. M. (2022). Developing and validating a combined attention systems test. Manuscript submitted for publication.

Lawrence, M. A. & Klein, R. M. (2013). Isolating exogenous and endogenous mechanisms of temporal attention. *Journal of Experimental Psychology: General*, 142 (2), 560–572.

Lu, Z. L. & Dosher, B. A. (2000). Spatial attention: Different mechanisms for central and peripheral temporal precues?. *Journal of Experimental Psychology: Human Perception and Performance*, 26 (5), 1534.

MacLeod, J. W., Lawrence, M. A., McConnell, M. M., Eskes, G. A., Klein, R. M. & Shore, D. I. (2010) Appraising the ANT: Psychometric and theoretical considerations of the Attention Network Test, *Neuropsychology*, 24 (5), 637–651.

Matthews, G., Warm, J. S., Reinerman, L. E., Langheim, L. K. & Saxby, D. J. (2010). Task engagement, attention, and executive control. In A. Gruszka, G. Matthews & B. Szymura (Eds.), *Handbook of individual differences in cognition*. Springer. https://doi.org/10.1007/978-1-4419-1210-7_13.

Matthews, G. & Zeidner, M. (2012). Individual differences in attentional networks: Trait and state correlates of the ANT. *Personality and Individual Differences*, 53 (5), 574–579. https://doi.org/10.1016/j.paid.2012.04.034.

McCormick, C. R., Redden, R. S., Lawrence, M. A. & Klein, R. M. (2018). The independence of endogenous and exogenous temporal attention. *Attention, Perception & Psychophysics*, 80 (8), 1885–1891.

McCormick, C. R. (2022). Lifestyle factors and their impact on the networks of attention. *Applied Cognitive Psychology*, 36 (1), 135–153.

Miller, G. A. (1956). The magical number seven, plus or minus two: Some limits on our capacity for processing information. *Psychological Review*, 63 (2), 81–97.

Mirsky, A. F., Anthony, B. J., Duncan, C. C., Ahearn, M. B. & Kellam, S. G. (1991) Analysis of the elements of attention: a neuropsychological approach. *Neuropsychology Review*, 2, 109–145 (1991).

Miyake, A., Friedman, N. P., Emerson, M. J., Witzki, A. H., Howerter, A. & Wager, T. D. (2000). The unity and diversity of executive functions and their contributions to complex "frontal lobe" tasks: A latent variable analysis. *Cognitive Psychology*, 41 (1), 49–100.

Mort, D. J., Perry, R. J., Mannan, S. K., Hodgson, T. L., Anderson, E., Quest, R., ... & Kennard, C. (2003). Differential cortical activation during voluntary and reflexive saccades in man. *Neuroimage*, 18 (2), 231–246.

Neisser, U. (1967). *Cognitive psychology*. Prentice-Hall.

Parasuraman, R. & Davies, D. (Eds.). (1984) *Varieties of attention*. Academic Press.

Petersen, S. E. & Posner, M. I. (2012). The attention system of the human brain: 20 years after. *Annual Review of Neuroscience*, 35, 73–89.

Posner, M. I. (1978). *Chronometric explorations of mind*. Lawrence Erlbaum.

Posner, M. I. (1980). Orienting of attention. *Quarterly Journal of Experimental Psychology*, 32, 3–25.

Posner, M. I. (1993). Interaction of arousal and selection in the posterior attention network. In A. Baddeley and L. Weiskrantz (eds.), *Attention: Selection, awareness and control. A tribute to Donald Broadbent*. Oxford University Press (pp. 390–405).

Posner, M. I. (Ed.). (2016). *The psychology of attention: vol 1. History of attention from ancient to modern times*. Routledge.

Posner, M. I. & Boies, S. J. (1971). Components of attention. *Psychological Review*, 78 (5), 391–408.

Posner, M. I., Nissen, M. J. & Ogden, W. C. (1978) Attended and unattended processing modes: The role of set for spatial location. In H. Pick (Ed.), *Modes of perceiving and processing information*. Lawrence Erlbaum Associates.

Posner, M. I. & Petersen, S.E., 1990. The attention system of the human brain. *Annual Review of Neuroscience* 13 (1), 25–42.

Posner, M. I., Rafal, R. D., Choate, L. S., & Vaughan, J. (1985). Inhibition of return: Neural basis and function. *Cognitive Neuropsychology*, 2(3), 211–228.

Posner, M. I. & Raichle, M. E. (1994). *Images of mind*. Scientific American Library/Scientific American Books.

Posner, M. I., Rothbart, M. K., Vizueta, N., Levy, K. N., Evans, D. E., Thomas, K. M. & Clarkin, J. F. (2002). Attentional mechanisms of borderline personality disorder. *Proceedings of the National Academy of Sciences*, 99(25), 16366–16370.

Posner, M. I. & Rothbart, M. K. (2007). Research on attention networks as a model for the integration of psychological science. *Annual Review of Psychology*, 58, 1–23.

Posner, M. I. & Snyder, C. R. R. (1975) Attention and cognitive control. In R. L. Solso (Ed.), *Information processing and cognition*. Lawrence Erlbaum Associates.

Posner, M. I., Snyder, C. R. R. & Davidson, B. J. (1980). Attention and the detection of signals. *Journal of Experimental Psychology: General*, 109, 160–174.

Prinzmetal, W., Presti, D. E. & Posner, M. I. (1986). Does attention affect visual feature integration?. *Journal of Experimental Psychology: Human Perception and Performance*, 12 (3), 361–369.

Puccetti, R. and Klein, R. M. (1980). Consciousness in contemporary psychology: Impressions of a conference. *Canadian Psychology*, 21, 179–184.

Raz, A. & Buhle, J. (2006). Typologies of attentional networks. *Nature Reviews Neuroscience*, 7 (5), 367–379.

Rescorla, R. A. (1967). Pavlovian conditioning and its proper control procedures. *Psychological Review*, 74(1), 71.

Reuter-Lorenz, P. A. & Fendrich, R. (1992). Oculomotor readiness and covert orienting: Differences between central and peripheral precues. *Perception and Psychophysics*, 52, 336–344.

Rueda, M. R., Fan, J., McCandliss, B. D., Halparin, J. D., Gruber, D. B., Lercari, L. P. & Posner, M. I. (2004). Development of attentional networks in childhood. *Neuropsychologia*, 42 (8), 1029–1040.

Shannon, C. E. (1948). A mathematical theory of communication. *The Bell System Technical Journal*, 27 (3), 379–423.

Simons, D. J. & Chabris, C. F. (1999). Gorillas in our midst: Sustained inattentional blindness for dynamic events. *Perception*, 28 (9), 1059–1074.

Sinha, N., Arora, S., Srivastava, P. & Klein, R. M. (2022). What networks of attention are affected by depression? A meta-analysis of studies that used the attention network test. *Journal of Affective Disorders Reports*, 8, 100302.

Sperling, G. (1960). The information available in brief visual presentations. *Psychological Monographs: General and Applied*, 74(11), 1.

Sperling, G. (1967). Successive approximations to a model for short term memory. *Acta Psychologica*, 27, 285–292.

Titchener, E. B. (1908) *Lectures on the elementary psychology of feeling and attention*. Macmillan.

Tolman, E. C. (1948). Cognitive maps in rats and men. *Psychological Review*, 55 (4), 189–208.

Treisman, A. T. & Gelade, G., (1980) A feature-integration theory of attention. *Cognitive Psychology*, 12 (1), 97–136.

Treisman, A. & Schmidt, H. (1982). Illusory conjunctions in the perception of objects. *Cognitive Psychology*, 14 (1), 107–141.

Tsal, Y. (1989). Do illusory conjunctions support the feature integration theory? A critical review of theory and findings. *Journal of Experimental Psychology: Human Perception and Performance*, 15 (2), 394–400.

Watson, J. B. (1913). Psychology as the behaviorist views it. *Psychological Review*, 20 (2), 158–177.

Wilson, M. (2002). Six views of embodied cognition. *Psychonomic Bulletin & Review*, 9 (4), 625–636.

3 Fractionating selection history

Dissociable components of experience-driven attention

Haena Kim and Brian A. Anderson

1 Traditional modes of attentional selection

Attentional selection refers to a shift of attention to a location with the highest priority. When sensory information enters the visual system, each location of a scene is assigned priority preattentively based on task goals and physical salience, forming a priority map. Attention then shifts to a location with the highest priority, biasing information processing at that location (Itti & Borji, 2014; Itti & Koch, 2001; Zelinsky & Bisley, 2015). When attention shifts to a location represented by a priority signal dominated by task goals, attentional selection is considered top-down or goal-directed. When attention shifts to a location with a priority signal dominated by physical salience, it is considered bottom-up or stimulus-driven. For example, to find your bag at an airport baggage reclaim, you need to keep in mind what your bag looks like and for each bag you see, determine whether it matches your bag. In this case, your attention is guided by top-down task goals to bags that share defining features with your searched-for bag. Most bags are rectangular and dark-shaded, yet some bags are brightly colored and/or have an irregular shape. These bags stand out from the rest and may attract your attention. Such attentional selection is guided by bottom-up physical salience. Below we discuss each mode of attentional selection in more detail.

1.1 Top-down attentional selection

Top-down attentional selection is guided by factors such as task goals and pre-existing knowledge. Based on such factors, observers shift their attention voluntarily. Such attentional selection operates slowly and has a sustained effect (Carrasco, 2011). Research in this domain has primarily focused on whether pre-existing knowledge of target locations and features can influence search performance. For example, in the endogenous cueing task, a central arrow indicates the likely location of the upcoming target. The target appears either at the location indicated by the arrow (valid location) or at uncued locations (invalid locations). Response times (RTs) to detect the target are faster on valid trials, because attention is directed towards the cued location and processing at that location is enhanced (Jonides, 1981; Posner, 1980). Attentional orienting is

DOI: 10.4324/9781003360896-3

top-down in this case, as observers need to process the meaning of the cue and voluntarily deploy attention to the cued location. Once directed, attention can be sustained until necessary.

Knowledge of target features can also improve performance by allowing observers to voluntarily direct attention to a particular feature/dimension (i.e., feature-based attention). Prominent theories of feature-based attention suggest that knowing the target feature allows observers to up-weight the expected feature, which enhances its relative salience, eventually facilitating detection of the target (Müller et al., 2003; Wolfe et al., 2003). For example, the Guided Search model proposes that an early, preattentive processor extracts basic features across the visual field in parallel and a later processor then subsequently assigns weights to the features based on task-relevance (Wolfe, 1994), which is maintained in working memory (Carlisle et al., 2011; Chelazzi et al., 1998; Desimone & Duncan, 1995). In situations which an observer has experienced in the past and therefore is familiar with, such task-relevant information may have developed via learning and are stored in long term memory (Cosman & Vecera, 2013; Leber & Egeth, 2006; Woodman et al., 2007). Consequently, task-relevant features receive enhanced representation in the priority map, making them more likely to be selected (Wolfe, 1994). Performance advantage for the cued feature/location is supported by the dorsal frontoparietal attentional network, which includes the frontal eye field (FEF) and posterior parietal cortex (Corbetta et al., 2008; Corbetta & Shulman, 2002; Hahn et al., 2006; Kincade et al., 2005). The dorsal attention network generates and maintains task goals and sends feedback to the visual cortex to modulate processing of locations and features that are consistent with these goals (Baluch & Itti, 2011; Battistoni et al., 2017; Chawla et al., 1999; Gazzaley & Nobre, 2012; Kastner et al., 1999).

1.2 Bottom-up attentional selection

Physically salient stimuli that have distinct attributes can attract attention in a bottom-up manner. Such attentional selection has a rapid onset and is transient (Carrasco, 2011; Donk & van Zoest, 2008). It happens involuntarily despite having a clear task goal that conflicts with prioritization of the salient stimulus and thus it is often referred to as attentional *capture* to reflect its reflexive nature. Research has focused on different aspects of salience, such as abrupt onset (e.g., Yantis & Jonides, 1984) and feature singleton (e.g., Theeuwes, 1992). In the well-known additional singleton task, observers search for a shape singleton target (e.g., circle) among non-target shapes (e.g., diamonds). All shapes generally appear in the same color, but occasionally, one of the non-target shapes appears in a unique color, making it a color singleton. On such trials, RTs to detect the shape singleton target slow down (Theeuwes, 1991, 1992). Eye movements have also been shown to be robustly biased in the direction of physically salient stimuli, with fixations occurring much more frequently on physically salient distractors compared to equally task-irrelevant but non-salient stimuli (Theeuwes et al., 2003; Theeuwes et al., 1998, 1999). This clearly demonstrates bottom-up attentional selection by the task-irrelevant color singleton that is rapid, transient and independent of task goals. The neural mechanism responsible for bottom-up attentional selection is the ventral frontoparietal network, including the right temporoparietal junction (TPJ) and inferior frontal cortex. Upon detection of a salient event, the ventral attention network alerts the need to shift attention to the salient event (Corbetta et al., 2008; Corbetta & Shulman, 2002), based on saliency signals represented in early visual areas (Beck & Kastner, 2005; Sprague et al., 2018).

2 Components of selection history

Selection history has been proposed recently to accommodate attentional selection that is neither top-down nor bottom-up (Awh et al., 2012). It refers to attentional selection based on prior experience of attending to a particular stimulus, independently of task goals and physical salience. Repeated experience with a stimulus changes its representation within the visual system (Desimone, 1996), granting it a competitive advantage within the priority map (Theeuwes, 2018). The contextual cueing effect is an example of attentional selection guided by selection history. In a visual search task, if a target appears at a particular location within a fixed spatial layout of distractors, search efficiency improves compared to unfamiliar search displays (Chun & Jiang, 1998). Across familiar and unfamiliar displays, the goals of the participants and the physical salience of the stimuli in the search array are equated, demonstrating an unequivocal effect of selection history in this case. Learned suppression constitutes another example of selection history. Repeated presentation of a distractor at a particular location results in reduced attentional processing at the location via statistical learning (Wang & Theeuwes, 2018). Among the different components of selection history that have been identified, this chapter will focus on the following: (1) reward history, (2) punishment history and (3) repeated selection as a target.

2.1 Reward history

In early research on reward and attention, reward was often tied to task demands. Observers were rewarded upon correct target detection, resulting in a performance benefit on reward target trials (e.g. Engelmann & Pessoa, 2007; Kiss et al., 2009). A limitation of such task design is that it is difficult to dissociate the top-down influence imposed by reward-related motivation and corresponding task goals versus any pure effect of reward on attention. Some studies tried to speak into this issue further by testing the effect of reward on attention in extinction, adopting a task design that has two separate phases—one for learning that a stimulus signals reward (i.e., reward history) and one for testing the effect of the reward signaling stimulus in the absence of reward delivery. They demonstrate that a stimulus that is rewarded during learning continues to be prioritized during test, such that it is preferentially selected (Della Libera & Chelazzi, 2009) and survives attentional blink (Raymond &

O'Brien, 2009) even when reward contingencies are removed. In these studies, however, the stimulus that is rewarded during learning remains task-relevant even during test (i.e., it continues to appear as a target), making it difficult to dislodge any effect of top-down reward-related motivation. A more informative task design would be one in which the task-relevant, rewarded stimulus during learning appears as a task-*irrelevant* item during test so that orienting to it is explicitly counterproductive. Only when the previously rewarded but now task-irrelevant item continues to bias attention can a study demonstrate a genuine effect of reward history per se on attention.

Anderson et al. (2011) adopts this approach. In their study, reward history is shaped via a training phase in which observers search for a specifically colored (e.g., red) circle and are awarded a monetary reward for correct performance. In a subsequent test phase, observers search for a circle among diamonds or vice versa, regardless of target color. Correct performance is no longer rewarded. Every shape is differently colored, and one of the non-target shapes sometimes appears in the color that defined the target in the training phase. This non-target shape is task-irrelevant and non-salient because the observers' goal is to find a unique shape and every item in the display has a different color. Therefore, there is no reason to orient to this non-target shape and doing so would only be counterproductive. Yet, on such occasions, RTs to detect the target shape slow down, suggesting that observers are automatically attracted to the non-target shape rendered in the previously rewarded color. Such attentional bias towards reward-signaling stimuli is referred to as value-driven attentional capture.

Research utilizing such task design has characterized how reward history influences attention. Although attentional bias towards reward-signaling stimuli is often referred to as value-driven attentional *capture*, implying that such stimuli are rapidly selected, they also delay attentional disengagement (Müller et al., 2016; Watson et al., 2020). Reward history can be shaped by a variety of reward types, including gustatory rewards and positive social feedback, and stimuli signaling these rewards all bias attention, just like monetary reward (Anderson, 2016; De Tommaso et al., 2017; Pool et al., 2014). Their effect to some degree scales with the reward magnitude, such that stimuli signaling higher reward bias attention to a greater extent (Anderson & Halpern, 2017; Le Pelley et al., 2015).

Importantly, reward history influences not only covert attention but also overt attention. In the presence of a reward signaling stimulus, saccades are generated faster and they land closer to the reward stimulus (Bucker et al., 2015a, 2015b). The effect of reward history on overt attention is pronounced especially in early saccades with short latencies, suggesting that value-driven attentional bias is automatic, just like attentional bias driven by physical salience (Anderson & Kim, 2019; Bucker et al., 2015a; Failing et al., 2015; Pearson et al., 2016). Indeed, reward-signaling stimuli receive enhanced representation in early visual areas (Hickey et al., 2010; Serences, 2008), and they attract attention even when doing so is counterproductive and despite explicit instructions to ignore them (Le Pelley et al., 2015; Pearson et al., 2015).

The effect of reward history is not limited to spatial selection (Failing & Theeuwes, 2014; Qi et al., 2013) but also extends to temporal selection. Task-irrelevant, non-salient reward stimuli that precede targets interfere with target processing (Failing & Theeuwes, 2015; Le Pelley et al., 2017, 2019). Finally, the effect of reward history is not limited to biases in the processing of sensory information but also extends to biased information processing in other cognitive domains including response selection and decision making. Reward-signaling stimuli evoke an accelerated reach motion with a more direct trajectory (Chapman et al., 2015; Painter et al., 2014) and such approach bias is resistant to top-down inhibition (Kim & Anderson, 2019c). When they are presented as an option that cannot be selected (i.e., as a distractor) in a decision-making context, they promote slower, suboptimal choices (Itthipuripat et al., 2015).

Research has also probed how an initially neutral stimulus acquires reward history and consequently biases attention. Learning of a stimulus-reward relationship involves an associative learning mechanism in which the stimulus comes to predict a rewarding outcome (Kim & Anderson, 2019a). After learning, the stimulus predictive of reward receives enhanced representation within the visual system (Anderson, 2017b; Itthipuripat et al., 2019; van Koningsbruggen et al., 2016), such that it grabs attention and elicits an approach bias (Berridge & Robinson, 1998). There are two mechanisms by which an initially neutral stimulus comes to predict reward and bias attention: (1) via plasticity in the visual cortex and (2) via the basal ganglia circuit. The first mechanism enhances effective salience of reward-signaling stimuli such that they receive heightened attentional priority within the visual system. The second mechanism contributes to the development of a habitual orienting response to such stimuli (Jiang, 2018; Jiang & Sisk, 2019; Le Pelley et al., 2016).

Repeatedly pairing a neutral stimulus with a reward enhances its representation within the visual system (Anderson, 2017b; Serences, 2008). Research has demonstrated that establishing a predictive relationship between the stimulus and reward is essential for developing the reward history that gives rise to subsequent attentional bias (Sali et al., 2014; Steinberg et al., 2013). Dopaminergic reward prediction error—the discrepancy between the actual reward and expected reward—serves as a teaching signal that drives visual plasticity (Arsenault et al., 2013; Roelfsema et al., 2010). A positive reward prediction error occurs when the actual reward is better than expected given a cue and it is indicated by an increase in the firing rate of midbrain dopamine neurons (Schultz et al., 1997). Early in learning, when a neutral stimulus is followed by an unexpected reward, a positive prediction error occurs, which updates reward-predictability of the stimulus. As learning progresses, the dopamine response to the reward transfers to the antecedent stimulus and it eventually comes to predict reward reliably (Glimcher, 2011; Sutton & Barto, 2018). After learning, the dopamine-tagged reward-signaling stimulus is preferentially represented in the visual cortex (Anderson, 2017b; Arsenault & Vanduffel, 2019; Serences, 2008), and competes with top-down and bottom-up attentional priority signals in the final priority map (Theeuwes, 2018).

Because reward-signaling stimuli receive enhanced representation in early sensory areas, reward salience is often likened to physical salience. Behaviorally, reward-signaling stimuli automatically capture attention just like physically salient stimuli (Anderson & Kim, 2019; Bucker et al., 2015a; Hickey et al., 2011; Wang et al., 2015) and they elicit early ERP components, suggesting that they influence early sensory processes (Donohue et al., 2016; Failing et al., 2015; Hickey et al., 2010; Kiss et al., 2009; Qi et al., 2013; San Martín et al., 2014). However, although reward-signaling and physically salient stimuli share a similar profile, there is evidence that they are not necessarily identical. Clearly, reward salience can robustly compete with physical salience in the process of attentional selection. Research has suggested that unlike physically salient stimuli which cannot break through an endogenous attentional focus, reward-signaling stimuli can do so (Munneke et al., 2016; Wang et al., 2014). Similarly, a top-down inhibitory mechanism can mitigate interference from physically salient stimuli but not that from reward-signaling stimuli (Pearson et al., 2020). A closer examination of the early ERP component N2pc revealed that whereas physically salient stimuli elicit N2pc with an earlier onset, which translates to earlier attentional selection, reward-signaling stimuli elicit N2pc with a larger amplitude, which evokes stronger attentional allocation (Bachman et al., 2020). Such added priority may originate from the basal ganglia circuit.

Attentional orienting towards reward-signaling stimuli can also arise as a consequence of value-based oculomotor decision making in the basal ganglia circuit (Hikosaka et al., 2019; Krauzlis et al., 2014), which may function independently of visual cortical mechanisms (Anderson, 2019; Kim et al., 2020; Sridharan et al., 2017; Takakuwa et al., 2017; Zénon & Krauzlis, 2012). The direct pathway, which encompasses inhibitory connections between the caudate nucleus, substantia nigra pars reticulata (SNr) and superior colliculus (SC), generates an orienting response towards reward-signaling stimuli (Hikosaka et al., 2014). A stimulus predictive of reward stimulates the caudate, which in turn inhibits the SNr. Inhibition of the inhibitory neurons in the SC (i.e., disinhibition) elicits an orienting response towards the reward-signaling stimulus.

Learning of a stimulus-reward association and generation of an orienting response thereafter is mediated in particular by a network of regions that includes the tail of the caudate nucleus and caudal-dorsolateral part of the SNr (cdlSNr), which guides behavior based on values that are learned over an extended period of time (Kim & Hikosaka, 2013; Yamamoto et al., 2013). Via learning, the caudate tail comes to discriminate stimuli that signal high- vs. low-value based on historic value information and generate saccades towards high-value stimuli by reducing cdlSNr-SC inhibition. Such value information is transmitted from dopamine neurons in the caudal-dorsolateral part of the substantia nigra pars compacta (cdlSNc). Importantly, the cdlSNc dopamine neurons are insensitive to moment-to-moment changes in stimulus-reward associations (i.e., they do not encode reward prediction error), but rather track long-term value information (Kim et al., 2014, 2015). Therefore, even after learning when reward delivery is no longer available, an organism continues to elicit an orienting response, suggesting that it is habitual. This view suggests that long-term reward learning does not depend on reward prediction errors, however, there exist alternative views which assume learning driven by reward prediction errors. Early in learning, a response is reinforced by dopaminergic reward signals and hence is goal-directed but with experience, it gradually becomes habitual (Tricomi et al., 2009; Wood & Rünger, 2016; Yin & Knowlton, 2006).

There is direct evidence from the attention literature that the basal ganglia circuit provides added priority and hence potentiates value-driven attentional capture. The magnitude of value-driven attentional capture is positively correlated with striatal dopaminergic activity (Anderson et al., 2016; Anderson et al., 2017b) and in particular, the caudate tail has been proposed as a marker of value-driven attentional capture (Anderson, 2019; Anderson et al., 2014a). There is some evidence that the amygdala also responds preferentially to previously reward-associated stimuli in a spatially-specific manner consistent with elevated attentional priority (Maeda et al., 2020; Peck et al., 2013; Peck & Salzman, 2014), although the role of the amygdala in the broader neutral networks supporting value-driven attention and its relation to behavioral indicators of attentional capture are less understood.

2.2 *Punishment history*

Similar to reward history, prior experience with aversive outcomes (i.e., punishment history) also influences attention. There is a robust literature examining attentional biases toward fear-related stimuli such as snakes, spiders and faces exhibiting fearful expressions (e.g., Fox et al., 2000; Öhman et al., 2001), although the role of selection history in such biases is unclear. To confidently link attentional biases for negatively valenced stimuli to selection history, it is necessary to manipulate stimulus-outcome associations in a similar manner to how reward is manipulated in the above-described studies.

Via associative learning, an initially neutral stimulus comes to predict an aversive outcome (Kim & Anderson, 2021a) and it continues to bias attention even when non-salient and task-irrelevant (Schmidt et al., 2015a; Wang et al., 2013; Wentura et al., 2014) and also delays attentional disengagement (Müller et al., 2016; Preciado et al., 2017; Schmidt et al., 2017). Aversively conditioned stimuli not only influence spatial selection but also temporal selection (Le Pelley et al., 2019). Punishment history can be shaped by a variety of aversive outcomes, including monetary loss (Müller et al., 2016; Wentura et al., 2014), electric shocks (Schmidt et al., 2015b, 2017), loud noise (Mikhael et al., 2021; Mulckhuyse, Crombez & Van der Stigchel, 2013), negative social feedback (Anderson, 2017a) and pain stimulation (Kim et al., 2021; L. Wang et al., 2013).

Punishment history also influences saccadic eye movements. Stimuli signaling aversive outcomes attract saccades, such that they facilitate selection when presented as targets but interfere when presented as distractors (Anderson & Britton, 2020; Hopkins et al., 2016; Mulckhuyse et al., 2013; Nissens et al., 2017; Schmidt et al., 2015b). Early saccades with short latencies are especially susceptible to the capture effect (Mulckhuyse et al., 2013; Nissens et al., 2017), suggesting that punishment history exerts an automatic influence on attention during early stages of sensory processing. Indeed, stimuli signaling aversive outcomes bias attention even when it is counterproductive to pay attention to them (Anderson & Britton, 2020; Mikhael et al., 2021; Nissens et al., 2017).

Given a similar behavioral profile between reward- and punishment-based attentional orienting, research has begun to examine whether they also share a similar neural profile. The midbrain regions commonly referred to as the "reward center" for their role in reward processing also play a role in processing aversive outcomes (Carter et al., 2009; Jensen et al., 2003; Liu et al., 2011; Oldham et al., 2018). These regions may possess salience-type dopamine neurons which respond to both reward and aversive outcomes (Bromberg-Martin et al., 2010; Horvitz, 2000; Matsumoto & Hikosaka, 2009) and thus possibly be involved in punishment-based attentional orienting. Indeed, research has shown that the salience-type dopamine neurons are located in the cdlSNc and they project to the caudate tail, which raises the possibility that punishment history-based attentional orienting develops and is generated via the same caudate tail-cdlSNr-SC pathway (Ghazizadeh et al., 2016; Hikosaka et al., 2019).

There are alternative views which argue that regional overlap does not necessitate a common mechanism of attentional orienting. It is possible that reward and aversive outcomes are represented along a bipolar continuum; the same regions are excited and suppressed in response to a rewarding outcome and aversive outcome, respectively (Barbaro et al., 2017; Delgado et al., 2000; Ilango et al., 2014; San Martín et al., 2014). This view is consistent with the traditional view on dopamine that they encode value signals (Schultz et al., 1997). Research has also identified anatomically separate brain regions for processing reward and aversive outcomes (e.g., Yacubian et al., 2006). Despite these alternatives, however, direct evidence from the attention literature has demonstrated that reward history and punishment history have similar influences on the attentional system, consistent with the motivational relevance model, which suggests that rather than a particular emotional valence, motivational salience is prioritized by the attentional system (Gable & Harmon-Jones, 2010; Kim et al., 2021). This and other evidence comparing the influence of reward and punishment history on the control of attention will be discussed in more detail in section 2.4. below.

2.3 History as a repeated target

Reward and punishment history involve repeatedly pairing a stimulus with either a reward or aversive outcome. However, such association with an outcome may not be necessary to produce the selection history effect; repeated exposure to a stimulus as a target may be sufficient to influence attention (Anderson et al., 2021; Awh et al., 2012). After an extensive training that spans multiple days in visual search for a particular stimulus, the stimulus comes to automatically attract attention even when non-salient and task-irrelevant (Kyllingsbæk et al., 2001, 2014; Qu et al., 2017; Schneider & Shiffrin, 1977). Slightly modifying the training phase used in Anderson et al. (2011) is also sufficient to produce the selection history effect. During training, observers repeatedly search for a particularly colored target but correct performance is not followed by explicit reward delivery for an extended period of time. In a subsequent test phase which involves searching for a unique shape, observers demonstrate an attentional bias toward the former target color (Kim & Anderson, 2019b).

Research on perceptual learning offers two possible mechanisms by which such selection history develops. Attention-gated learning suggests that attention mediates selection and learning of relevant information by enhancing signals that are task-relevant so they are better learned and suppressing those that are task-irrelevant so they do not interfere with learning of task-relevant information (Sasaki et al., 2010; Tsushima et al., 2008). Performance feedback can facilitate learning, but it is not necessary (Petrov et al., 2006; Shiu & Pashler, 1992). This suggests that in the training task described above, a correct response requires orienting to the target and such attentional orienting towards the target boosts its representation, which potentiates plasticity within the visual cortex.

Alternatively, learning may be driven by reward signals that serve as a teaching signal to the visual system. Explicit reward delivery after successful performance generates reward prediction error signals, which reinforce visual features that are present in the scene and drive learning (Seitz et al., 2009). Internal rewards have the same effect; upon successful performance, a sense of accomplishment generates an internal reward signal which facilitates visual plasticity (Sasaki et al., 2010; Seitz et al., 2005). Similar to explicit rewards, such internal reward signals evoke striatal activation, which reflects prediction error based on performance confidence (i.e., discrepancy between the level of confidence in performance on a given trial and the expected level of performance confidence based on previous experiences; Daniel & Pollmann, 2012). If this learning mechanism underlies repetition history-based attentional capture, then its neural profile should be similar to that of value-driven attentional capture. Contrary to this account, however, as will be described in more detail in the following section, Kim and Anderson (2019b) did not observe activation in the caudate tail despite behavioral evidence that former targets capture attention. Rather, it appears that attentional bias towards former targets is due to their enhanced representation in the visual cortex.

2.4 Relationship among different components of selection history

Research in the attention field has largely focused on identifying different components of selection history. How they are related and together influence attentional orienting are beginning to be explored. One dominant view in the field suggests that selection history is a unitary construct; different components of selection history are the products of a common learning mechanism based on statistical regularities (Failing & Theeuwes, 2018; Theeuwes, 2019). In other words, this view assumes that different components of selection history are fundamentally identical in nature but represented as different sources of attentional bias. If they are fundamentally identical, then it follows that they would interact to be integrated into a single source of bias and jointly guide attention. However, growing evidence suggests that they are distinct and hence exert independent influences on the attentional system. Below we discuss how the three components of selection history—(1) reward history, (2) punishment history and (3) history as a repeated target—are related and propose that they collectively reflect two distinct sources of bias that have independent influences on the attentional system.

Research on how reward learning and aversive conditioning influence attentional orienting has garnered evidence that the attentional system follows the motivational relevance model; it may be guided primarily by motivational salience, rather than a particular emotional valence (Gable & Harmon-Jones, 2010). Both reward and aversive outcomes provide critical information for survival and hence elicit an automatic attentional orienting response that facilitates reward/threat detection and allows preparation of an appropriate action (Elliot & Covington, 2001; LeDoux, 1996; Vuilleumier, 2005).

Consistent with the model, stimuli signaling reward and aversive outcomes capture attention even when non-salient and task-irrelevant (e.g., Anderson et al., 2011; Schmidt et al., 2015a). In both instances, the same brain regions within the frontoparietal attentional network and dopaminergic midbrain structures are involved. In particular, the caudate tail has been identified as the marker of attentional capture by reward and aversive outcomes (Anderson et al., 2014a). Importantly, stimuli that signal reward and aversive outcomes evoke a similar pattern of activation within these regions (Kim et al., 2021; Lindquist et al., 2016). Given that most research up to date uses financial incentives which are secondary reinforcers for reward learning and electric shocks which are primary punishers for aversive conditioning, one may question the validity of the argument that reward and punishment history have similar influences on the attentional system. A study that matched for reinforcer/punisher dimensions using primary tastes has confirmed that appetitive and aversive outcomes indeed bias attention in a similar manner (Kim & Anderson, 2023).

In addition, both reward and punishment history develop via Pavlovian associative learning in which a stimulus–stimulus (S-S) association develops, rather than instrumental learning which results in a response–outcome (R-O) association. In other words, an organism learns that a stimulus predicts a reward/aversive outcome, rather than that an orienting response results in a reward/aversive outcome (Kim & Anderson, 2019a, 2021b). This has been shown using the anti-saccade training task, in which a colored probe appears either on the left or right of a central fixation cross and observers are instructed to look the opposite direction as soon as possible. Observers are rewarded for correctly looking away from the probe. Two possible relationships can develop as a result of this training: (1) an S-S association where the probe color predicts a reward and thus attention is biased towards the reward-signaling probe, and (2) an R-O association where the orienting response is associated with a reward. The probe would not attract overt attention in this case. In a subsequent test phase, a circle target and a square distractor appear simultaneously on each side and observers are instructed to fixate the circle target. The distractor occasionally appears in the previously rewarded color. Although during the anti-saccade training task, observers are rewarded for shifting gaze away from the probe, attention is nevertheless biased towards the reward-signaling distractor in the test phase, as evidenced by slower RTs when the distractor appears in the previously rewarded color. Such results demonstrate that associative learning plays a dominant role in value-driven attentional capture (Kim & Anderson, 2019a; see also Le Pelley et al., 2015). A similar pattern of results were obtained when reward was replaced with shocks, suggesting that also in the case of threat-driven attentional capture, associative learning primarily guides the attentional system (Kim & Anderson, 2021b).

While reward and punishment history share a common learning mechanism and have analogous influences on the attentional system, they are fundamentally distinct from history as a repeated target. Behaviorally, all three histories bias attention in a similar manner after learning (e.g., Anderson et al., 2011; Kim & Anderson, 2019b; Kim et al., 2021), which may lead to a conclusion that they constitute a unitary construct. However, a similar behavioral profile does not warrant a similar neural profile. Attentional bias based on reward and punishment history involves the dopaminergic midbrain structures, notably the caudate tail (Anderson, et al., 2014a; Kim et al., 2021). Yet, development of repetition history and its subsequent influence on the attentional system is primarily driven by plasticity within the visual cortex (Kim & Anderson, 2019b).

Reward/punishment history and target repetition history emerge via distinct learning mechanisms, which adds to the claim that they are distinct sources of bias. Whereas reward and punishment history develop via associative learning, repetition history does not engage associative learning. The same anti-saccade training task described above but without reward/aversive outcome delivery provides support for this claim. If associative learning plays a role in the development of repetition history, then in the same subsequent test phase, attention should be attracted to the distractor rendered in the former probe color and slow down RTs. Contrary to this hypothesis, however, attention is not biased toward the distractor rendered in the former probe color; instead, RTs are faster in this case, suggesting that observers develop a habitual gaze shift away from the probe during the training phase (Kim & Anderson, 2019a).

Additional evidence in support of dissociable learning mechanisms comes from patients with depression, who exhibit dysfunctional reward processing. The reward learning task used in Anderson et al. (2011) failed to produce value-driven attentional capture in depression patients (Anderson et al., 2014b). However, after completing the same learning task for an extended period of time but without reward feedback, depressed participants showed attentional bias towards former target-colored distractors, suggesting that the learning mechanism that generates history as a repeated target is intact in these patients and that reward/punishment history and repetition history rely on dissociable learning mechanisms (Anderson et al., 2017a).

Furthermore, while the stimulus-reward (Anderson, 2015) and stimulus-punishment (Grégoire et al., 2021) associations that bias attention are learned in a context-dependent manner, attentional biases toward former target features arises in a manner that is insensitive to the context in which they are experienced during training (Anderson & Britton, 2019).

Learned suppression is another component of selection history not discussed in the present review. However it deserves a brief discussion, as its relationship with reward and punishment history demonstrates that different components of selection history have independent influences on the attentional system. Learned suppression arises as a result of repeated presentation of a salient distractor at a particular location. Doing so results in reduced attentional processing at that location. Consequently, search is facilitated when a distractor appears at the location but impaired when a target appears at the location (Wang & Theeuwes, 2018; see also Britton & Anderson, 2020). A recent study examined whether reward-signaling stimuli can overcome such learned suppression. In a training phase, observers were trained to suppress a particular location (high probability location) and associate colors with reward or no outcome (neutral). In a subsequent test phase, reward and neutral distractors appeared in all locations equally often. Results showed that reward distractors captured attention more strongly than neutral distractors irrespective of their location. Distractors appearing in the high probability location showed reduced capture irrespective of their type. Replacing reward with electric shocks produced an identical pattern of results, indicating that reward and punishment history exert similar influences on the attentional system, and that learned suppression and reward/punishment history are independent sources of bias (Kim & Anderson, 2021a).

3 Conclusions

In this chapter, we provide an overview of three different components of selection history, how they are related, and the mechanism by which they influence the attentional selection. The three components—(1) reward history (2) punishment history and (3) history as a repeated target—all bias attention independently of task goals and physical salience, which is broadly consistent with the idea that they constitute a unitary construct. This view claims that the different components share the same origin—statistical regularities—and thus are fundamentally identical with respect to how they influence attention. Therefore, they would interact and jointly guide attention via a common underlying mechanism (Failing & Theeuwes, 2018; Theeuwes, 2019).

However, a closer examination suggests otherwise. While reward and punishment history share a similar profile, history as a repeated target has unique characteristics that differentiate it from the two, providing support for independent sources of bias. This view claims that reward/punishment history and history as a repeated target reflect distinct sources of bias and thus each would independently guide attention.

Indeed, the field has seen growing evidence for the independent sources of bias account. Reward and punishment history, although the former is positively valenced and the latter is negatively valenced, both bias attention in a similar manner and arise via the same associative learning mechanism (Kim & Anderson, 2019a, 2021b). They not only share a common behavioral profile but also a common neural profile. Attentional bias towards reward and aversive outcomes recruits the dopaminergic midbrain structures, in particular, the caudate tail, and the pattern of neural responses across the brain are indistinguishable (Kim et al., 2021). These findings imply that the attentional system is guided primarily by motivational salience, rather than a particular valence. Unlike reward and punishment history, history as a repeated target arises via an instrumental learning mechanism (Kim & Anderson, 2019a). Attentional orienting towards former targets does not recruit the dopaminergic midbrain structures. Rather, priority is afforded by attention-gated plasticity within the visual cortex, which results in enhanced representation of such stimuli (Kim & Anderson, 2019b).

This clear distinction between reward and punishment history on one hand and history as a repeated target on the other, together with more recent evidence that pits these sources of bias directly against each other (Kim & Anderson, 2021a) unequivocally suggests that different components of selection history reflect distinct sources of bias that are not integrated through a single (unitary) representation of learning-dependent priority but maintain their independence until they reach a common (general) priority map.

4 Questions for future research

- What are the mechanisms by which different sources of experience-dependent attentional priority are integrated in the brain and combine with other influences on attentional priority?
- What are the mechanisms by which experience-dependent attentional biases contribute to approach and avoidance behavior?
- How are experience-dependent prioritization and suppression (Kim & Anderson, 2021a) related mechanistically, and how are they different?
- What are the mechanisms by which statistical learning shapes the control of attention, and how do they relate to the components of selection history discussed in this chapter?
- How can an understanding of the role of selection history in the control of attention be used to strategically curb attentional biases through targeted training?

References

Anderson, B. A. (2015). Value-driven attentional priority is context specific. *Psychonomic Bulletin & Review*, 22(3), 750–756.

Anderson, B. A. (2016). Social reward shapes attentional biases. *Cognitive Neuroscience*, 7(1–4),30–36.

Anderson, B. A. (2017a). Counterintuitive effects of negative social feedback on attention. *Cognition and Emotion*, 31(3), 590–597.

Anderson, B. A. (2017b). Reward processing in the value-driven attention network: reward signals tracking cue identity and location. *Social Cognitive and Affective Neuroscience*, 12(3), 461–467.

Anderson, B. A. (2019). Neurobiology of value-driven attention. *Current Opinion in Psychology*, 29, 27–33.

Anderson, B. A. & Britton, M. K. (2019). Selection history in context: Evidence for the role of reinforcement learning in biasing attention. *Attention, Perception & Psychophysics*, 81(8), 2666–2672.

Anderson, B. A. & Britton, M. K. (2020). On the automaticity of attentional orienting to threatening stimuli. *Emotion*, 20, 1109–1112.

Anderson, B. A., Chiu, M., DiBartolo, M. M. & Leal, S. L. (2017a). On the distinction between value-driven attention and selection history: Evidence from individuals with depressive symptoms. *Psychonomic Bulletin & Review*, 24(5), 1636–1642.

Anderson, B. A. & Halpern, M. (2017). On the value-dependence of value-driven attentional capture. *Attention, Perception & Psychophysics*, 79(4), 1001–1011.

Anderson, B. A. & Kim, H. (2019). On the relationship between value-driven and stimulus-driven attentional capture. *Attention, Perception & Psychophysics*, 81(3), 607–613.

Anderson, B. A., Kim, H., Kim, A. J., Liao, M.-R., Mrkonja, L., Clement, A. & Gregoire, L. (2021). The past, present, and future of selection history. *Neuroscience and Biobehavioral Reviews*, 130, 326–350.

Anderson, B. A., Kuwabara, H., Wong, D. F., Gean, E. G., Rahmim, A., Brašić, J. R., ... Yantis, S. (2016). The Role of Dopamine in Value-Based Attentional Orienting. *Current Biology*, 26(4), 550–555.

Anderson, B. A., Kuwabara, H., Wong, D. F., Roberts, J., Rahmim, A., Brašić, J. R. & Courtney, S. M. (2017b). Linking dopaminergic reward signals to the development of attentional bias: A positron emission tomographic study. *Neuroimage*, 157, 27–33.

Anderson, B. A., Laurent, P. A. & Yantis, S. (2011). Value-driven attentional capture. *Proceedings of the National Academy of Sciences*, 108(25), 10367–10371.

Anderson, B. A., Laurent, P. A. & Yantis, S. (2014a). Value-driven attentional priority signals in human basal ganglia and visual cortex. *Brain Research*, 1587, 88–96.

Anderson, B. A., Leal, S. L., Hall, M. G., Yassa, M. A. & Yantis, S. (2014b). The attribution of value-based attentional priority in individuals with depressive symptoms. *Cognitive, Affective & Behavioral Neuroscience*, 14(4), 1221–1227.

Arsenault, John T., Nelissen, K., Jarraya, B. & Vanduffel, W. (2013). Dopaminergic reward signals selectively decrease fMRI activity in primate visual cortex. *Neuron*, 77 (6), 1174–1186.

Arsenault, J. T. & Vanduffel, W. (2019). Ventral midbrain stimulation induces perceptual learning and cortical plasticity in primates. *Nature Communications*, 10(1), 3591.

Awh, E., Belopolsky, A. V. & Theeuwes, J. (2012). Top-down versus bottom-up attentional control: a failed theoretical dichotomy. *Trends in Cognitive Sciences*, 16(8), 437–443.

Bachman, M. D., Wang, L., Gamble, M. L. & Woldorff, M. G. (2020). Physical salience and value-driven salience operate through different neural mechanisms to enhance attentional selection. *The Journal of Neuroscience*, 40(28), 5455–5464.

Baluch, F. & Itti, L. (2011). Mechanisms of top-down attention. *Trends in Neurosciences*, 34(4), 210–224.

Barbaro, L., Peelen, M. V. & Hickey, C. (2017). Valence, not utility, underlies reward-driven prioritization in human vision. *The Journal of Neuroscience*, 37(43), 10438.

Battistoni, E., Stein, T. & Peelen, M. V. (2017). Preparatory attention in visual cortex. *Annals of the New York Academy of Sciences*, 1396(1), 92–107.

Beck, D. M. & Kastner, S. (2005). Stimulus context modulates competition in human extrastriate cortex. *Nature Neuroscience*, 8(8), 1110–1116.

Berridge, K. C. & Robinson, T. E. (1998). What is the role of dopamine in reward: hedonic impact, reward learning, or incentive salience? *Brain Research Reviews*, 28(3), 309–369.

Britton, M. K. & Anderson, B. A. (2020). Specificity and persistence of statistical learning in distractor suppression. *Journal of Experimental Psychology: Human Perception and Performance*, 46, 324–334.

Bromberg-Martin, E. S., Matsumoto, M. & Hikosaka, O. (2010). Dopamine in motivational control: Rewarding, aversive, and alerting. *Neuron*, 68(5), 815–834.

Bucker, B., Belopolsky, A. V. & Theeuwes, J. (2015a). Distractors that signal reward attract the eyes. *Visual Cognition*, 23(1–2), 1–24.

Bucker, B., Silvis, J. D., Donk, M. & Theeuwes, J. (2015b). Reward modulates oculomotor competition between differently valued stimuli. *Vision Research*, 108, 103–112.

Carlisle, N. B., Arita, J. T., Pardo, D. & Woodman, G. F. (2011). Attentional templates in visual working memory. *The Journal of Neuroscience*, 31(25), 9315.

Carrasco, M. (2011). Visual attention: The past 25 years. *Vision Research*, 51(13), 1484–1525.

Carter, R. M., MacInnes, J., Huettel, S. & Adcock, R. A. (2009). Activation in the VTA and nucleus accumbens increases in anticipation of both gains and losses. *Frontiers in Behavioral Neuroscience*, 3(21).

Chapman, C. S., Gallivan, J. P. & Enns, J. T. (2015). Separating value from selection frequency in rapid reaching biases to visual targets. *Visual Cognition*, 23(1–2), 249–271.

Chawla, D., Rees, G. & Friston, K. J. (1999). The physiological basis of attentional modulation in extrastriate visual areas. *Nature Neuroscience*, 2(7), 671–676.

Chelazzi, L., Duncan, J., Miller, E. K. & Desimone, R. (1998). Responses of neurons in inferior temporal cortex during memory-guided visual search. *Journal of Neurophysiology*, 80(6), 2918–2940.

Chun, M. M. & Jiang, Y. (1998). Contextual cueing: Implicit learning and memory of visual context guides spatial attention. *Cognitive Psychology*, 36(1), 28–71.

Corbetta, M., Patel, G. & Shulman, G. L. (2008). The reorienting system of the human brain: From environment to theory of mind. *Neuron*, 58(3), 306–324.

Corbetta, M. & Shulman, G. L. (2002). Control of goal-directed and stimulus-driven attention in the brain. *Nature Reviews Neuroscience*, 3, 201.

Cosman, J. D. & Vecera, S. P. (2013). Context-dependent control over attentional capture. *Journal of Experimental Psychology: Human Perception and Performance*, 39(3), 836–848.

Daniel, R. & Pollmann, S. (2012). Striatal activations signal prediction errors on confidence in the absence of external feedback. *Neuroimage*, 59(4), 3457–3467.

De Tommaso, M., Mastropasqua, T. & Turatto, M. (2017). The salience of a reward cue can outlast reward devaluation. *Behavioral Neuroscience*, 131(3), 226–234.

Delgado, M. R., Nystrom, L. E., Fissell, C., Noll, D. C. & Fiez, J. A. (2000). Tracking the hemodynamic responses to reward and punishment in the striatum. *Journal of Neurophysiology* 84(6), 3072–3077.

Della Libera, C. & Chelazzi, L. (2009). Learning to attend and to ignore is a matter of gains and losses. *Psychological Science*, 20(6), 778–784.

Desimone, R. (1996). Neural mechanisms for visual memory and their role in attention. *Proceedings of the National Academy of Sciences*, 93(24), 13494.

Desimone, R. & Duncan, J. (1995). Neural mechanisms of selective visual attention. *Annual Review of Neuroscience*, 18(1), 193–222.

Donk, M. & van Zoest, W. (2008). Effects of salience are short-lived. *Psychological Science*, 19(7), 733–739.

Donohue, S. E., Hopf, J.-M., Bartsch, M. V., Schoenfeld, M. A., Heinze, H.-J. & Woldorff, M. G. (2016). The rapid capture of attention by rewarded objects. *Journal of Cognitive Neuroscience*, 28(4), 529–541.

Elliot, A. J. & Covington, M. V. (2001). Approach and avoidance motivation. *Educational Psychology Review*, 13(2), 73–92.

Engelmann, J. B. & Pessoa, L. (2007). Motivation sharpens exogenous spatial attention. *Emotion*, 7(3), 668–674.

Failing, M., Nissens, T., Pearson, D., Le Pelley, M. E. & Theeuwes, J. (2015). Oculomotor capture by stimuli that signal the availability of reward. *Journal of Neurophysiology*, 114(4), 2316–2327.

Failing, M. & Theeuwes, J. (2014). Exogenous visual orienting by reward. *Journal of Vision*, 14(5), 6.

Failing, M. & Theeuwes, J. (2015). Nonspatial attentional capture by previously rewarded scene semantics. *Visual Cognition*, 23(1–2), 82–104.

Failing, M. & Theeuwes, J. (2018). Selection history: How reward modulates selectivity of visual attention. *Psychonomic Bulletin & Review*, 25(2), 514–538.

Fox, E., Lester, V., Russo, R., Bowles, R. J., Pichler, A. & Dutton, K. (2000). Facial expressions of emotion: Are angry faces detected more efficiently? *Cognition and Emotion*, 14(1), 61–92.

Gable, P. & Harmon-Jones, E. (2010). The motivational dimensional model of affect: Implications for breadth of attention, memory, and cognitive categorisation. *Cognition and Emotion*, 24(2), 322–337.

Gazzaley, A. & Nobre, A. C. (2012). Top-down modulation: bridging selective attention and working memory. *Trends in Cognitive Sciences*, 16(2), 129–135.

Ghazizadeh, A., Griggs, W. & Hikosaka, O. (2016). Ecological origins of object salience: Reward, uncertainty, aversiveness, and novelty. *Frontiers in Neuroscience*, 10(378).

Glimcher, P. W. (2011). Understanding dopamine and reinforcement learning: The dopamine reward prediction error hypothesis. *Proceedings of the National Academy of Sciences*, 108(Supplement 3), 15647.

Grégoire, L., Kim, H. & Anderson, B. A. (2021). Punishment-modulated attentional capture is context specific. *Motivation Science*, 7(2), 165–175.

Hahn, B., Ross, T. J. & Stein, E. A. (2006). Neuroanatomical dissociation between bottom–up and top–down processes of visuospatial selective attention. *Neuroimage*, 32(2), 842–853.

Hickey, C., Chelazzi, L. & Theeuwes, J. (2010). Reward changes salience in human vision via the anterior cingulate. *The Journal of Neuroscience*, 30(33), 11096.

Hickey, C., Chelazzi, L. & Theeuwes, J. (2011). Reward has a residual impact on target selection in visual search, but not on the suppression of distractors. *Visual Cognition*, 19(1), 117–128.

Hikosaka, O., Kim, H. F., Amita, H., Yasuda, M., Isoda, M., Tachibana, Y. & Yoshida, A. (2019). Direct and indirect pathways for choosing objects and actions. *European Journal of Neuroscience*, 49(5), 637–645.

Hikosaka, O., Kim, H. F., Yasuda, M. & Yamamoto, S. (2014). Basal ganglia circuits for reward value–guided behavior. *Annual Review of Neuroscience*, 37(1), 289–306.

Hopkins, L. S., Helmstetter, F. J. & Hannula, D. E. (2016). Eye movements are captured by a perceptually simple conditioned stimulus in the absence of explicit contingency knowledge. *Emotion*, 16(8), 1157–1171.

Horvitz, J. C. (2000). Mesolimbocortical and nigrostriatal dopamine responses to salient non-reward events. *Neuroscience*, 96(4), 651–656.

Ilango, A., Kesner, A. J., Keller, K. L., Stuber, G. D., Bonci, A. & Ikemoto, S. (2014). Similar roles of substantia nigra and ventral tegmental dopamine neurons in reward and aversion. *The Journal of Neuroscience*, 34(3), 817.

Itthipuripat, S., Cha, K., Rangsipat, N. & Serences, J. T. (2015). Value-based attentional capture influences context-dependent decision-making. *Journal of Neurophysiology*, 114(1), 560–569.

Itthipuripat, S., Vo, V. A., Sprague, T. C. & Serences, J. T. (2019). Value-driven attentional capture enhances distractor representations in early visual cortex. *PLOS Biology*, 17(8), e3000186.

Itti, L. & Borji, A. (2014). Computational models: Bottom-up and top-down aspects. In A. C. Nobre & S. Kastner (Eds.), *The Oxford handbook of attention*. Oxford University Press.

Itti, L. & Koch, C. (2001). Computational modelling of visual attention. *Nature Reviews Neuroscience*, 2(3), 194–203.

Jensen, J., McIntosh, A. R., Crawley, A. P., Mikulis, D. J., Remington, G. & Kapur, S. (2003). Direct activation of the ventral striatum in anticipation of aversive stimuli. *Neuron*, 40(6), 1251–1257.

Jiang, Y. V. (2018). Habitual versus goal-driven attention. *Cortex*, 102, 107–120.

Jiang, Y. V. & Sisk, C. A. (2019). Habit-like attention. *Current Opinion in Psychology*, 29, 65–70.

Jonides, J. (1981). Voluntary versus automatic control over the mind's eye's movement. In J. Long & A. D. Baddeley (Eds.), *Attention & performance* (Vol. 9, pp. 187–203). Erlbaum.

Kastner, S., Pinsk, M. A., De Weerd, P., Desimone, R. & Ungerleider, L. G. (1999). Increased activity in human visual cortex during directed attention in the absence of visual stimulation. *Neuron*, 22(4), 751–761.

Kim, H. & Anderson, B. A. (2019a). Dissociable components of experience-driven attention. *Current Biology*, 29(5), 841–845.

Kim, H. & Anderson, B. A. (2019b). Dissociable neural mechanisms underlie value-driven and selection-driven attentional capture. *Brain Research*, 1708, 109–115.

Kim, H. & Anderson, B. A. (2019c). Neural evidence for automatic value-modulated approach behaviour. *Neuroimage*, 189, 150–158.

Kim, H. & Anderson, B. A. (2021a). Combined influence of valence and statistical learning on the control of attention: Evidence for independent sources of bias. *Cognition*, 208, 104554.

Kim, H. & Anderson, B. A. (2021b). How does the attention system learn from aversive outcomes? *Emotion*, 21(4), 898–903.

Kim, H. & Anderson, B. A. (2023). Primary rewards and aversive outcomes have comparable effects on attentional bias. *Behavioral Neuroscience*, 137(2), 89–94.

Kim, H., Nanavaty, N., Ahmed, H., Mathur, V. A. & Anderson, B. A. (2021). Motivational salience guides attention to valuable and threatening stimuli: Evidence from behavior and functional magnetic resonance imaging. *Journal of Cognitive Neuroscience*, 1–21.

Kim, H. F., Ghazizadeh, A. & Hikosaka, O. (2014). Separate groups of dopamine neurons innervate caudate head and tail encoding flexible and stable value memories. *Frontiers in Neuroanatomy*, 8(120).

Kim, H. F., Ghazizadeh, A. & Hikosaka, O. (2015). Dopamine neurons encoding long-term memory of object value for habitual behavior. *Cell*, 163(5), 1165–1175.

Kim, H. F., Griggs, W. S. & Hikosaka, O. (2020). Long-term value memory in the primate posterior thalamus for fast automatic action. *Current Biology*, 30(15), 2901–2911.e2903.

Kim, H. F. & Hikosaka, O. (2013). Distinct basal ganglia circuits controlling behaviors guided by flexible and stable values. *Neuron*, 79(5), 1001–1010.

Kincade, J. M., Abrams, R. A., Astafiev, S. V., Shulman, G. L. & Corbetta, M. (2005). An event-related functional magnetic resonance imaging study of voluntary and stimulus-driven orienting of attention. *Journal of Neuroscience*, 25(18), 4593–4604.

Kiss, M., Driver, J. & Eimer, M. (2009). Reward priority of visual target singletons modulates event-related potential signatures of attentional selection. *Psychological Science*, 20(2), 245–251.

Krauzlis, R. J., Bollimunta, A., Arcizet, F. & Wang, L. (2014). Attention as an effect not a cause. *Trends in Cognitive Sciences*, 18(9), 457–464.

Kyllingsbæk, S., Schneider, W. X. & Bundesen, C. (2001). Automatic attraction of attention to former targets in visual displays of letters. *Perception & Psychophysics*, 63(1), 85–98.

Kyllingsbæk, S., Van Lommel, S., Sørensen, T. A. & Bundesen, C. (2014). Automatic attraction of visual attention by supraletter features of former target strings. *Frontiers in Psychology*, 5, 1383.

Le Pelley, M. E., Mitchell, C. J., Beesley, T., George, D. N. & Wills, A. J. (2016). Attention and associative learning in humans: An integrative review. *Psychological Bulletin*, 142(10), 1111–1140.

Le Pelley, M. E., Pearson, D., Griffiths, O. & Beesley, T. (2015). When goals conflict with values: Counterproductive attentional and oculomotor capture by reward-related stimuli. *Journal of Experimental Psychology: General*, 144(1), 158–171.

Le Pelley, M. E., Seabrooke, T., Kennedy, B. L., Pearson, D. & Most, S. B. (2017). Miss it and miss out: Counterproductive nonspatial attentional capture by task-irrelevant, value-related stimuli. *Attention, Perception & Psychophysics*, 79(6), 1628–1642.

Le Pelley, M. E., Watson, P., Pearson, D., Abeywickrama, R. S. & Most, S. B. (2019). Winners and losers: Reward and punishment produce biases in temporal selection. *Journal of Experimental Psychology: Learning, Memory, and Cognition*, 45(5), 822–833.

Leber, A. B. & Egeth, H. E. (2006). Attention on autopilot: Past experience and attentional set. *Visual Cognition*, 14(4–8), 565–583.

LeDoux, J. E. (1996). *The emotional brain: The mysterious underpinnings of emotional life*. Simon & Schuster.

Lindquist, K. A., Satpute, A. B., Wager, T. D., Weber, J. & Barrett, L. F. (2016). The brain basis of positive and negative affect: Evidence from a meta-analysis of the human neuroimaging literature. *Cerebral Cortex*, 26(5), 1910–1922.

Liu, X., Hairston, J., Schrier, M. & Fan, J. (2011). Common and distinct networks underlying reward valence and processing stages: A meta-analysis of functional neuroimaging studies. *Neuroscience & Biobehavioral Reviews*, 35(5), 1219–1236.

Maeda, K., Inoue, K.-i., Kunimatsu, J., Takada, M. & Hikosaka, O. (2020). Primate amygdalo-nigral pathway for boosting oculomotor action in motivating situations. *iScience*, 23(6).

Matsumoto, M. & Hikosaka, O. (2009). Two types of dopamine neuron distinctly convey positive and negative motivational signals. *Nature*, 459(7248), 837–841.

Mikhael, S., Watson, P., Anderson, B. A. & Le Pelley, M. E. (2021). You do it to yourself: Attentional capture by threat-signaling stimuli persists even when entirely counterproductive. *Emotion*, 21(8), 1691–1698.

Mulckhuyse, M., Crombez, G. & Van der Stigchel, S. (2013). Conditioned fear modulates visual selection. *Emotion*, 13(3), 529–536.

Müller, H. J., Reimann, B. & Krummenacher, J. (2003). Visual search for singleton feature targets across dimensions: Stimulus- and expectancy-driven effects in dimensional weighting. *Journal of Experimental Psychology: Human Perception and Performance*, 29(5), 1021–1035.

Müller, S., Rothermund, K. & Wentura, D. (2016). Relevance drives attention: Attentional bias for gain- and loss-related stimuli is driven by delayed disengagement. *Quarterly Journal of Experimental Psychology*, 69(4), 752–763.

Munneke, J., Belopolsky, A. V. & Theeuwes, J. (2016). Distractors associated with reward break through the focus of attention. *Attention, Perception & Psychophysics*, 78(7), 2213–2225.

Nissens, T., Failing, M. & Theeuwes, J. (2017). People look at the object they fear: oculomotor capture by stimuli that signal threat. *Cognition and Emotion*, 31(8), 1707–1714.

Öhman, A., Flykt, A. & Esteves, F. (2001). Emotion drives attention: Detecting the snake in the grass. *Journal of Experimental Psychology: General*, 130(3), 466–478.

Oldham, S., Murawski, C., Fornito, A., Youssef, G., Yücel, M. & Lorenzetti, V. (2018). The anticipation and outcome phases of reward and loss processing: A neuroimaging meta-analysis of the monetary incentive delay task. *Human Brain Mapping*, 39(8), 3398–3418.

Painter, D. R., Kritikos, A. & Raymond, J. E. (2014). Value learning modulates goal-directed actions. *Quarterly Journal of Experimental Psychology*, 67(6), 1166–1175.

Pearson, D., Donkin, C., Tran, S. C., Most, S. B. & Le Pelley, M. E. (2015). Cognitive control and counterproductive oculomotor capture by reward-related stimuli. *Visual Cognition*, 23(1–2), 41–66.

Pearson, D., Osborn, R., Whitford, T. J., Failing, M., Theeuwes, J. & Le Pelley, M. E. (2016). Value-modulated oculomotor capture by task-irrelevant stimuli is a consequence of early competition on the saccade map. *Attention, Perception & Psychophysics*, 78(7), 2226–2240.

Pearson, D., Watson, P., Cheng, P. & Le Pelley, M. E. (2020). Overt attentional capture by reward-related stimuli overcomes inhibitory suppression. *Journal of Experimental Psychology: Human Perception and Performance*, 46(5), 489–501.

Peck, C. J., Lau, B. & Salzman, C. D. (2013). The primate amygdala combines information about space and value. *Nature Neuroscience*, 16(3), 340–348.

Peck, C. J. & Salzman, C. D. (2014). Amygdala neural activity reflects spatial attention towards stimuli promising reward or threatening punishment. *eLife*, 3, e04478.

Petrov, A. A., Dosher, B. A. & Lu, Z.-L. (2006). Perceptual learning without feedback in non-stationary contexts: Data and model. *Vision Research*, 46(19), 3177–3197.

Pool, E., Brosch, T., Delplanque, S. & Sander, D. (2014). Where is the chocolate? Rapid spatial orienting toward stimuli associated with primary rewards. *Cognition*, 130(3), 348–359.

Posner, M. I. (1980). Orienting of attention. *Quarterly Journal of Experimental Psychology*, 32(1), 3–25.

Preciado, D., Munneke, J. & Theeuwes, J. (2017). Was that a threat? Attentional biases by signals of threat. *Emotion*, 17(3), 478–486.

Qi, S., Zeng, Q., Ding, C. & Li, H. (2013). Neural correlates of reward-driven attentional capture in visual search. *Brain Research*, 1532, 32–43.

Qu, Z., Hillyard, S. A. & Ding, Y. (2017). Perceptual learning induces persistent attentional capture by nonsalient shapes. *Cerebral Cortex*, 27(2), 1512–1523.

Raymond, J. E. & O'Brien, J. L. (2009). Selective visual attention and motivation: The consequences of value learning in an attentional blink task. *Psychological Science*, 20(8), 981–988.

Roelfsema, P. R., van Ooyen, A. & Watanabe, T. (2010). Perceptual learning rules based on reinforcers and attention. *Trends in Cognitive Sciences*, 14(2), 64–71.

Sali, A. W., Anderson, B. A. & Yantis, S. (2014). The role of reward prediction in the control of attention. *Journal of Experimental Psychology: Human Perception and Performance*, 40(4), 1654–1664.

San Martín, R., Appelbaum, L. G., Huettel, S. A. & Woldorff, M. G. (2014). Cortical brain activity reflecting attentional biasing toward reward-predicting cues covaries with economic decision-making performance. *Cerebral Cortex*, 26(1), 1–11.

Sasaki, Y., Nanez, J. E. & Watanabe, T. (2010). Advances in visual perceptual learning and plasticity. *Nature Reviews Neuroscience*, 11(1), 53–60.

Schmidt, L. J., Belopolsky, A. V. & Theeuwes, J. (2015a). Attentional capture by signals of threat. *Cognition and Emotion*, 29(4), 687–694.

Schmidt, L. J., Belopolsky, A. V. & Theeuwes, J. (2015b). Potential threat attracts attention and interferes with voluntary saccades. *Emotion*, 15(3), 329–338.

Schmidt, L. J., Belopolsky, A. V. & Theeuwes, J. (2017). The time course of attentional bias to cues of threat and safety. *Cognition and Emotion*, 31(5), 845–857.

Schneider, W. & Shiffrin, R. M. (1977). Controlled and automatic human information processing: I. Detection, search, and attention. *Psychological Review*, 84(1), 1–66.

Schultz, W., Dayan, P. & Montague, P. R. (1997). A neural substrate of prediction and reward. *Science*, 275(5306), 1593.

Seitz, A., Kim, D. & Watanabe, T. (2009). Rewards evoke learning of unconsciously processed visual stimuli in adult humans. *Neuron*, 61(5), 700–707.

Seitz, A., Lefebvre, C., Watanabe, T. & Jolicoeur, P. (2005). Requirement for high-level processing in subliminal learning. *Current Biology*, 15(18), R753–R755.

Serences, J. T. (2008). Value-based modulations in human visual cortex. *Neuron*, 60(6), 1169–1181.

Shiu, L.-P. & Pashler, H. (1992). Improvement in line orientation discrimination is retinally local but dependent on cognitive set. *Perception & Psychophysics*, 52(5), 582–588.

Sprague, T. C., Itthipuripat, S., Vo, V. A. & Serences, J. T. (2018). Dissociable signatures of visual salience and behavioral relevance across attentional priority maps in human cortex. *Journal of Neurophysiology*, 119(6), 2153–2165.

Sridharan, D., Steinmetz, N. A., Moore, T. & Knudsen, E. I. (2017). Does the superior colliculus control perceptual sensitivity or choice bias during attention? Evidence from a multialternative decision framework. *The Journal of Neuroscience*, 37(3), 480.

Steinberg, E. E., Keiflin, R., Boivin, J. R., Witten, I. B., Deisseroth, K. & Janak, P. H. (2013). A causal link between prediction errors, dopamine neurons and learning. *Nature Neuroscience*, 16(7), 966–973.

Sutton, R. S. & Barto, A. G. (2018). *Reinforcement learning: An introduction*. MIT Press.

Takakuwa, N., Kato, R., Redgrave, P. & Isa, T. (2017). Emergence of visually-evoked reward expectation signals in dopamine neurons via the superior colliculus in V1 lesioned monkeys. *eLife*, 6, e24459.

Theeuwes, J. (1991). Cross-dimensional perceptual selectivity. *Perception & Psychophysics*, 50(2), 184–193.

Theeuwes, J. (1992). Perceptual selectivity for color and form. *Perception & Psychophysics*, 51(6), 599–606.

Theeuwes, J. (2010). Top–down and bottom–up control of visual selection. *Acta Psychologica*, 135(2), 77–99.

Theeuwes, J. (2018). Visual selection: Usually fast and automatic; seldom slow and volitional. *Journal of Cognition*, 1(1).

Theeuwes, J. (2019). Goal-driven, stimulus-driven, and history-driven selection. *Current Opinion in Psychology*, 29, 97–101.

Theeuwes, J., de Vries, G.-J. & Godijn, R. (2003). Attentional and oculomotor capture with static singletons. *Perception & Psychophysics*, 65(5), 735–746.

Theeuwes, J., Kramer, A. F., Hahn, S. & Irwin, D. E. (1998). Our eyes do not always go where we want them to go: Capture of the eyes by new objects. *Psychological Science*, 9(5), 379–385.

Theeuwes, J., Kramer, A. F., Hahn, S., Irwin, D. E. & Zelinsky, G. J. (1999). Influence of attentional capture on oculomotor control. *Journal of Experimental Psychology: Human Perception and Performance*, 25(6), 1595–1608.

Tricomi, E., Balleine, B. W. & O'Doherty, J. P. (2009). A specific role for posterior dorsolateral striatum in human habit learning. *European Journal of Neuroscience*, 29 (11), 2225–2232.

Tsushima, Y., Seitz, A. R. & Watanabe, T. (2008). Task-irrelevant learning occurs only when the irrelevant feature is weak. *Current Biology*, 18(12), R516–R517.

van Koningsbruggen, M. G., Ficarella, S. C., Battelli, L. & Hickey, C. (2016). Transcranial random-noise stimulation of visual cortex potentiates value-driven attentional capture. *Social Cognitive and Affective Neuroscience*, 11(9), 1481–1488.

Vuilleumier, P. (2005). How brains beware: neural mechanisms of emotional attention. *Trends in Cognitive Sciences*, 9(12), 585–594.

Wang, B. & Theeuwes, J. (2018). Statistical regularities modulate attentional capture. *Journal of Experimental Psychology: Human Perception and Performance*, 44(1), 13–17.

Wang, L., Duan, Y., Theeuwes, J. & Zhou, X. (2014). Reward breaks through the inhibitory region around attentional focus. *Journal of Vision*, 14(12), 2.

Wang, L., Yu, H., Hu, J., Theeuwes, J., Gong, X., Xiang, Y., … Zhou, X. (2015). Reward breaks through center-surround inhibition via anterior insula. *Human Brain Mapping*, 36(12), 5233–5251.

Wang, L., Yu, H. & Zhou, X. (2013). Interaction between value and perceptual salience in value-driven attentional capture. *Journal of Vision*, 13(3), 5.

Watson, P., Pearson, D., Theeuwes, J., Most, S. B. & Le Pelley, M. E. (2020). Delayed disengagement of attention from distractors signalling reward. *Cognition*, 195, 104125.

Wentura, D., Müller, P. & Rothermund, K. (2014). Attentional capture by evaluative stimuli: Gain- and loss-connoting colors boost the additional-singleton effect. *Psychonomic Bulletin & Review*, 21(3), 701–707.

Wolfe, J. M. (1994). Guided Search 2.0 A revised model of visual search. *Psychonomic Bulletin & Review*, 1(2), 202–238.

Wolfe, J. M., Butcher, S. J., Lee, C. & Hyle, M. (2003). Changing your mind: On the contributions of top-down and bottom-up guidance in visual search for feature singletons. *Journal of Experimental Psychology: Human Perception and Performance*, 29(2), 483–502.

Wood, W. & Rünger, D. (2016). Psychology of habit. *Annual Review of Psychology*, 67 (1), 289–314.

Woodman, G. F., Luck, S. J. & Schall, J. D. (2007). The role of working memory representations in the control of attention. *Cerebral Cortex*, 17(suppl_1), i118–i124.

Yacubian, J., Gläscher, J., Schroeder, K., Sommer, T., Braus, D. F. & Büchel, C. (2006). Dissociable systems for gain- and loss-related value predictions and errors of prediction in the human brain. *The Journal of Neuroscience*, 26(37), 9530.

Yamamoto, S., Kim, H. F. & Hikosaka, O. (2013). Reward value-contingent changes of visual responses in the primate caudate tail associated with a visuomotor skill. *The Journal of Neuroscience*, 33(27), 11227.

Yantis, S. & Jonides, J. (1984). Abrupt visual onsets and selective attention: Evidence from visual search. *Journal of Experimental Psychology: Human Perception and Performance*, 10(5), 601–621.

Yin, H. H. & Knowlton, B. J. (2006). The role of the basal ganglia in habit formation. *Nature Reviews Neuroscience*, 7(6), 464–476.

Zelinsky, G. J. & Bisley, J. W. (2015). The what, where, and why of priority maps and their interactions with visual working memory. *Annals of the New York Academy of Sciences*, 1339(1), 154–164.

Zénon, A. & Krauzlis, R. J. (2012). Attention deficits without cortical neuronal deficits. *Nature*, 489(7416), 434–437.

4 Attentional guidance and priority maps

Dominique Lamy, Daniel Toledano and Aniruddha Ramgir

In this chapter, we first explain how the theoretical concept of a priority map emerged in attention research and briefly describe brain areas suggested as candidate priority maps (section 1). We then describe the different types of information thought to determine attentional priority (section 2) and reevaluate previous attempts at hierarchizing these (section 3). Finally, we note that theories that have developed around the concept of a priority map have typically ignored insights from research on temporal attention, and therefore do not fully account for how information is dynamically prioritized in space and time. We present a preliminary attempt to achieve such integration, the Priority Accumulation Framework (section 4).

1 The concept of a priority map

1.1 The priority map in conceptual models of attention

The main precursor of the concept of a priority map is Koch and Ullman's (1985) "Saliency Map" model. According to the model, the saliency map is an explicit two-dimensional topographical map that encodes stimulus saliency at every location of the visual scene. Saliency is determined primarily by how different the visual input in a particular location is from its neighbors on each feature dimension (e.g., color or depth). The saliency map combines the outputs from all feature maps into a global saliency index for each location. Thus, an important characteristic of the saliency map is that it is not feature-specific: it codes saliency per se, and not the features that drive saliency (i.e., it is indifferent to whether the peak of activation is a horizontal line among vertical ones or a black patch among white ones). At any given time, attention is moved to the location with the highest activation on the saliency map, in a winner-take-all fashion. This location is then inhibited to allow attention to move on to the next highest location (inhibition of return, Posner & Cohen, 1984). Thus, based on the premise that perceptually salient locations are worthy candidates for attentional selection, the model assumes that locations in a visual scene are scanned in descending order of saliency.

Although Treisman and Gelade (1980) were among the first to introduce the concept of a feature-blind central map serving as the representational

DOI: 10.4324/9781003360896-4

medium for selection. Treisman's "master map of locations" can hardly qualify as a "priority" map. According to Treisman's Feature Integration Theory (FIT) in its initial form, the presence of an object differing from all its neighbors on a given dimension can be detected during a preattentive stage of processing by monitoring activation on separate feature maps that code basic features in parallel. When the search task requires conjoining different features into bound objects, the attentional "beam" must be focused on the master map to retrieve and bind feature information, and locations on the map are serially scanned. Importantly, activations on the map only signal filled locations: they do not constrain the probability that any given location will receive attention.

The next development in the concept of a priority map came as a criticism of Treisman's FIT. Wolfe, Cave and Franzel (1989) argued that search is seldom random, as assumed by FIT. Instead, it is guided by the observers' knowledge of how the target they are searching for looks like. To account for this influence, Wolfe and colleagues suggested the Guided Search model, which differs from FIT mainly in the interaction between the parallel and serial stages. The model posits that during the parallel stage, the match with the target feature (top-down component) and local contrast (bottom-up component) are computed for each location and separately for each feature dimension. The outputs of the computations from each feature dimension are summed to produce an overall activation map, with the activation level at each location indexing how likely this location is to receive attention. To find the target participants successively attend to the locations represented on the activation (or priority) map, in descending order of activation value. Thus, unlike the Saliency model (Koch & Ullman, 1985) Guided Search includes a top-down component and does not assume an overall saliency map combining bottom-up activations across dimensions (as top-down and bottom-up influences are combined for each feature dimension map). Since the pioneering work of Cave and Wolfe (1990), most models of attention posit a role for both bottom-up and top-down guidance (e.g., Anderson et al., 2021; Desimone & Duncan, 1995; Luck et al., 2021; Navalpakkam & Itti, 2005; Wolfe, 2021).

Although the concept of a priority map is common to many models of attention, other models do not assume the existence of a map that explicitly codes priority. Among the most influential is Desimone and Duncan's (1995) Biased Competition model. This model posits that objects in the world compete for representation in the brain: when several stimuli are presented within a neuron's receptive field, this neuron's response is largely driven by the stimulus to which the animal is instructed to attend. Importantly, competition in favor of a given stimulus is biased not only through top-down feedback signals but also its local salience (bottom-up attention). Attentional priority manifests as stronger neural responses to some stimuli at the expense of others throughout the hierarchy of visual maps and is therefore an emergent property of neural activity across a distributed network of neural maps, with no map or group of maps dedicated to indexing priority.

1.2 Priority maps in the brain

While conceptual models of attention typically assume one general priority map, brain studies have identified several candidate priority-maps. What properties are required for a neural representation to qualify as a priority map? Zelinsky and Bisley (2015) define a priority map as "a neural representation of a topographic space in which activity codes for the priority of locations in that space irrespective of the bottom-up or top-down factors contributing to this prioritization" (p. 3; see also Liesefeld et al., 2024). Similarly, White et al. (2017) distinguish between a saliency map which codes overall saliency across feature dimensions at each location, and a priority map which combines activations on this saliency map with top-down signals. These authors emphasize that to qualify as a saliency or as a priority map, a map should show little or no feature-related preference.

Despite some controversy (e.g., Bisley & Mirpour, 2019; Serences & Kastner, 2014; for reviews), several maps seem to fulfil these criteria, in particular, the superior colliculus (SC, e.g., Thompson, Bichot & Schall, 1997; with different roles for the intermediate and superficial layers, SCi and SCs, respectively, e.g., White et al., 2017), the frontal eye-field (FEF, e.g., Kustov & Lee Robinson, 1996), and the lateral interparietal sulcus (LIP, e.g., Gottlieb, Kusunoki & Goldberg, 1998). All three maps are thought to guide both covert and overt attention, but their respective roles have been debated. For instance, Zelinsky and Bisley (2015) proposed a common source hypothesis, by which "there may be only one prioritization of a goal, with the different priority maps throughout the brain existing mainly to interact with different effector systems" (p. 8). Relatedly, Bisley and Mirpour (2019) suggested that LIP provides a simple representation of attentional priority, while FEF controls the flow and timing of saccades based on the input from LIP, and the intermediate layers of the superior colliculus (SCi) index the final saccade goal. By contrast, White et al. (2017) suggested that SCs serves as a saliency map that feeds into SCi, where goal-irrelevant visual inputs are suppressed to determine which salient signals gain access to the downstream attentional and gaze systems. Thus, how the LIP, SCi, SCs and FEF interact to determine the location of highest priority in our visual field remains an active research topic.

Authors who adopt Desimone and Duncan's (1995) Biased Competition model (e.g., Serences & Kastner, 2014; Sprague et al., 2018) suggest a rather different and more general definition of the priority maps: any spatial map where activation levels are correlated with the importance of an object in a given situation is a priority map. They posit that "both visual salience and behavioral relevance dissociably influence the activity profile across retinotopic cortex to compute an attentional priority map within each region" and that "each region's priority map will weight these factors to varying degrees" (Sprague et al., 2018, p. 2153). Accordingly, because they assume attentional allocation to be an emergent property of the competition across the visual hierarchy, they claim that "attentional priority maps are ubiquitous and span subcortical areas, as well as occipital, temporal, parietal and frontal cortex" (Serences & Kastner, 2014, p. 177). This use of the term "priority map" is confusing, however, because it deprives the concept of one of its central characteristics: the requirement that it should code *only* the priority accruing to each object and be insensitive to featural information. It thereby conflates neural maps that are affected by attention with maps that determine where our attention will go next.

To summarize, the notion of a priority map has emerged early in conceptual models of selective attention and has become pervasive in thinking about how we prioritize objects in our visual field at the expense of others. Subsequent research has corroborated the existence of one or several priority maps in the midbrain, parietal cortex and frontal cortex, yet their respective roles and the interplay between them remain to be established.[1] Other maps are also sometimes referred to as priority maps because processing in these maps is influenced by attention, yet to avoid confusion, we suggest that the term should be reserved for representations that code only the relative importance of locations in the visual field, based on the input from several sources of attentional guidance, with no sensitivity to the features of these objects.

2 Beyond the bottom-up vs. top-down dichotomy

2.1 *A fuzzy line between bottom-up and top-down factors*

One major recent development in the study of attentional allocation is the diversification of the factors thought to guide attention. Up to the 2000s, most models posited only bottom-up and top-down influences on attentional priority. However, what these terms cover became contentious (as Egeth and Yantis, 1997 warned presciently, when they advocated using the terms "salience-driven" and "goal-directed" instead of "bottom-up" and "top-down", respectively).

The controversy initially revolved around intertrial priming effects. These refer to the performance benefit of repeating vs. changing a feature of the target or distractors (e.g., Maljkovic & Nakayama, 1994; Lamy et al., 2008a), the target-defining-dimension (e.g., Found & Müller, 1996), the target location (e.g., Maljkovic & Nakayama, 1996; see Toledano & Lamy, in press for a review), or the status of the target as a singleton (e.g., Lamy, Bar-Anan & Egeth, 2008b) on successive visual search trials. For instance, when the target is unpredictably either the red diamond among green ones or the green diamond among red ones (i.e., the unique- color object, whatever its color), search is faster when the target and distractors color repeat than when they swap on consecutive trials. These repetitions speed search substantially and reliably, and there is increasing evidence that they modulate the priority of the repeated stimulus aspect rather than only post-selective processes (see Ramgir & Lamy, 2021 for a review).

However, whether intertrial priming should be held to operate in a "bottom-up" or "top-down" fashion became controversial. On the one hand, Theeuwes

(2018) affirmed that because intertrial priming effects are independent of the observers' intentions (Maljkovic & Nakayama, 1994; but see Cochrane & Pratt, 2020), their influence should be counted as bottom-up. He went further to claim that most effects attributed to top-down guidance merely reflect such intertrial priming (e.g., Belopolsky, Schreij & Theeuwes, 2010; see Lamy & Kristjánsson, 2013 for a review). On the other hand, adopting the definition of top-down processes that prevails in the perception domain, namely, "knowledge, expectations, or past experiences that shape the interpretation of sensory information" (Gazzaniga, Heatherton & Halpern, 2016, p. 173), other authors affirmed that the influence of intertrial priming should count as top-down (e.g., Egeth, 2018). To resolve this semantic controversy, we suggest that search goals should be distinguished from selection history (but that both influence attentional priority top-down).

2.2 Selection history as a separate source of attentional guidance

Beyond intertrial priming, the influence of past experience on attentional priority have been documented through a variety of phenomena, such as contextual cueing (e.g., Chun & Jiang, 1998), probability cueing (e.g., Geng & Behrmann, 2005), reward (e.g., Anderson et al., 2011), statistical learning of distractor location (e.g., Wang & Theeuwes, 2018; Ferrante et al., 2018) or feature (e.g., Stilwell, Bahle & Vecera, 2019) and scene-based guidance (e.g., Torralba et al., 2006). These influences are assumed to be implicit (e.g., Jiang, 2018; but see Vadillo et al., 2020), long-lasting (e.g., Golan & Lamy, 2022a) and to be resistant to explicit instructions (e.g., Golan & Lamy, 2022b)—three characteristics that distinguish guidance by past experience from goal-directed guidance.

As a result, most researchers agree that the effects of past experience on visual search should be distinguished from stimulus-driven and goal-directed effects and grouped under a third category typically called *selection history* (e.g., Liesefeld et al., 2024; Lamy, Amunts & Bar-Haim, 2008; see Figure 4.1; but see Gimenez-Fernandez et al., 2023 for a different view). Within this framework, stimulus-driven guidance refers exclusively to increased priority accruing to physically salient stimuli. Goal-directed guidance refers to increased priority to objects matching the properties defined by implicit or explicit momentary task goals. Selection history encompasses relatively short-term effects of individual past search episodes (intertrial priming), longer-term effects of ad-hoc statistical regularities with regard to the target's or distractors' properties or with regard to the relation between them (statistical learning), effects of statistical regularities learned over a life-time (e.g., scene-based guidance) and long-term effects of learned value (guidance related to features previously associated with reward or punishment).

Conceptual models of attentional priority differ in how exactly they group the different selection-history phenomena. For instance, Awh et al. (2012) suggested just one selection-history category including a myriad of phenomena, the core feature of which is that "past selection episodes are recapitulated in

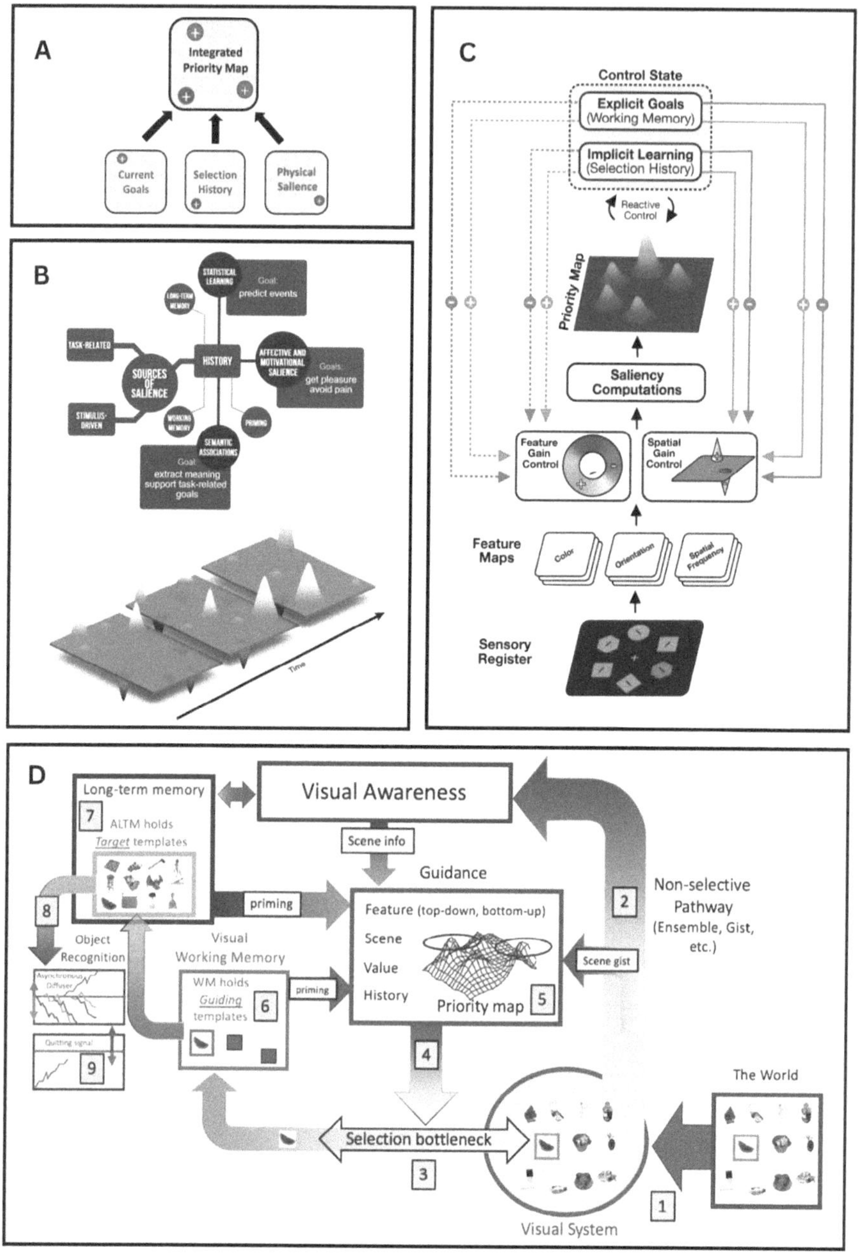

Figure 4.1 Sources of attentional guidance converging into the priority map in different attention models.

Sources: reproduced with permission from (a) Awh et al. (2012), (b) Todd and Manaligod (2018), (c) Luck et al. (2021) and (d) Wolfe (2021) subsequent trials when the relevant context is encountered again" (p.4). By contrast, Anderson et al. (2021) proposed a three-component classification (associations with valent outcomes, statistical learning and stimulus-response habit learning) that can produce long-lasting attentional biases or short-term intertrial priming effects. This classification relies on a variety of dissociations, notably on the extent to which the three components depend on context.

To summarize, most current models of attention agree that three sources of attentional guidance combine to determine where we will shift our attention next: stimulus salience, momentary goals and selection history, a category that encompasses a variety of dissociable influences of past experience on attentional priority.

3 A hierarchy among sources of guidance?

How do the various sources of guidance (stimulus salience, momentary goals and the various types of selection history) combine to shape the priority map? The assumption that is implicit in most attention models is that at any given moment, a weighted average of the various sources of guidance determines where we attend next (Wolfe, 2021), with the relative contributions of each of these sources changing according to the task context (e.g., Todd & Manaligod, 2018). A direct implication of this view is that none of the guiding factors deserves a special status and that there is no fixed hierarchy among them. Thus, for instance, a salient irrelevant object (e.g., an abruptly onset distractor) might receive attention first when it happens to appear at the location of a previously attended target but might lose the competition to an object with a task-relevant shape when it appears elsewhere.

However, as we explain in the next two sections, two lines of research challenge this simple model. First, several authors have suggested that the different mechanisms affect attentional priority in qualitatively different ways. Second, despite the recently achieved consensus that stimulus salience, goals and selection history all affect activations on the priority map, claims that one source of guidance overrides the others are often voiced.

3.1 Qualitatively different influences on attentional selection?

3.1.1 Early vs. late influences on the priority map

One widely entertained idea is that stimulus-driven guidance is faster than goal-directed guidance (e.g., van Heusden et al., 2022; van Zoest, Donk & Theeuwes, 2004; see also Anderson, 2019 for a similar claim with regard to value-driven guidance). For instance, Müller and Rabbitt (1989) showed that the effect of a central spatial cue (i.e., an informative arrow pointing in a given direction on a trial-by-trial basis) peaks at around 400 ms, whereas the effect of a peripheral cue (i.e., a brief non-informative flash in the periphery of the visual field) peaks much earlier, at around 100 ms. However, this finding only indicates that establishing a task goal takes time and that if a salient event occurs before this process is completed, it will summon attention. The finding is mute as to whether stimulus salience prevails early on when task goals are already established.

In later studies, to allow participants to set up their task goals early in practice, these were required to make a speeded saccade towards a target defined by the same known feature across the experiment (e.g., van Heusden et al., 2022; van Zoest, Donk & Theeuwes, 2004). The results showed that fast saccades were completely stimulus driven whereas goal-driven control dominated only later. The authors concluded that "visual selection is not necessarily the outcome of a direct battle between saliency- and relevance-driven signals... and the time at which an action is initiated determines which of the two will emerge as the driving force of behavior" (van Heusden et al., 2022, p. 1327).

However, in these studies the target was defined as a feature discontinuity, thereby encouraging salience-based search (or "singleton-detection mode", Bacon & Egeth, 1994). According to this account, slow saccades correspond to trials in which participants were able to refrain from moving their eyes to the first attended (most salient) object (the distractor) and waited until they redirected their attention to the next most salient object (the target); fast saccades correspond to trials in where such control failed. To test this alternative account, it would be important to investigate whether the mapping of early and fast saccades onto stimulus-driven and goal-directed guidance is replicated with tasks that force participants to search for a specific feature (i.e., feature-search mode, Bacon & Egeth, 1994) and using free-viewing rather than speeded saccade tasks.

Challenging the notion that salience-driven guidance is faster than goal-directed guidance, several studies have shown that advance knowledge of the target feature generates a baseline shift (e.g., Beck et al., 2012) – enhanced activity of populations of neurons coding that feature, even before the search display appears. These findings indicate that feature-based goal-directed attention can prioritize processing of target-matching stimuli proactively.

To conclude, there is no convincing evidence, to date, that goal-directed prioritization of a feature lags behind stimulus-directed prioritization.

3.1.2 A special status for goal-directed guidance by location?

Many researchers agree that spatial information deserves a special status in attentional allocation (see Lamy & Tsal, 2000 for review). In particular, studies showed that when attention is focused on a location (for instance, by a 100%-valid precue presented long enough for attention to zoom in onto the cued location), salient events occurring elsewhere do not capture attention (e.g., Theeuwes, 1991; Yantis & Jonides, 1990).

To account for these findings, Theeuwes (e.g., 1991; 2004) has claimed that priority computations contribute to determine where attention is shifted next only within the attentional window, the size of which can be strategically adjusted as a function of expected search difficulty (see also Eriksen & St James, 1986). When attention is distributed across the visual field, the most salient object will receive attention, whereas tightly focusing attention on a specific location prevents distraction.

However, several studies invalidate this claim (e.g., Folk et al., 2002; Lamy et al., 2004). In these studies, participants searched for a color-defined letter in a rapid serial visual presentation stream at fixation. They did not know *when* but knew with certainty *where* the target would appear and could therefore focus their attention there. Yet, a target-colored distractor at a peripheral location 5° away from center captured attention. These findings clearly demonstrate that focusing attention on a narrow location in not sufficient for preventing an involuntary shift of attention away from this location and challenge the special status often attributed to goal-directed guidance to locations.

3.1.3 Separate pathways for attentional selection

A different suggestion is that some sources of guidance may affect attentional priority through a rapid, direct pathway that bypasses the general priority map. For instance, Anderson et al. (2021) proposed that there exist

> two signaling pathways underlying value-based attentional priority, one biasing competition in a spatial priority map (as hypothesized by Awh et al., 2012) and another biasing rapid and automatic eye movements more directly through a pathway encompassing the visual cortex, caudate tail, and superior colliculus.
>
> (Anderson et al. (2021, p. 338)

In a similar vein, Jiang (2018) suggested a distinction between habitual shifts of attention and shifts determined by activation levels on the general priority map. She suggested that

> attention also has a procedural component—the *how* component of spatial attention. Visual search, for example, involves frequent shifts of spatial attention from one location to another. Every time a target is successfully detected, the most recent shifts of attention that lead to target detection are reinforced, increasing the likelihood that such vectors of attentional shift would occur again.
>
> (Jiang, 2018, p. 116)

This dual-system view of how spatial attention is implemented can readily account for statistical learning phenomena involving learned associations with a specific target location (e.g., probability cueing, Geng & Behrmann, 2005; contextual cueing, Chun & Jiang, 1998). However, further research is needed determine whether habitual attention can account for intertrial priming as well as for selection history phenomena involving traces of previously selected *features* rather than *locations*.

These suggestions raise the possibility that at any given moment, a race might occur for the control of attention between learned habits that elicit reflexive attention shifts to a location and computations on the priority map that designate a winning location. Testing this idea and how different learned habits combine is an important avenue for future research.

3.2 What is attentional capture?

3.2.1 Fewer discrepancies than meet the eye

Despite the proclaimed consensus among most contenders in the so-called "attentional capture debate" around the idea that salience, goals and selection history jointly affect attentional guidance (e.g., Luck et al. 2021), claims that one source of attentional guidance overrides another remain vocal. For instance, Pearson et al. (2020) claimed that

> reward related stimuli constitute especially potent attentional priority signals that are not only immune to volitional attentional control (e.g., Pearson et al., 2015), but are also relatively immune to suppression by nonvolitional inhibitory control processes that can act to prevent distraction by physical salience.
> (Pearson et al., 2020, p. 498)

Likewise, Wang and Theeuwes (2020) and Stilwell and Gaspelin (2021) have recently argued over whether feature-based suppression overrides stimulus salience or vice versa. Feature-based suppression refers to a mechanism by which the attentional priority of a potentially distracting feature is reduced through repeated experience (e.g., Vatterott & Vecera, 2012) or based on previous knowledge of this feature (e.g., Arita et al., 2012), thereby preventing attentional capture by that feature. It is worth describing these studies in some detail in order to illustrate the type of inferences that prevail in the attentional-capture literature, and how these can explain enduring disagreements.

Both studies relied on the capture-probe paradigm (Figure 4.2). In that paradigm, on most (search) trials participants respond to a shape-defined target (e.g., a

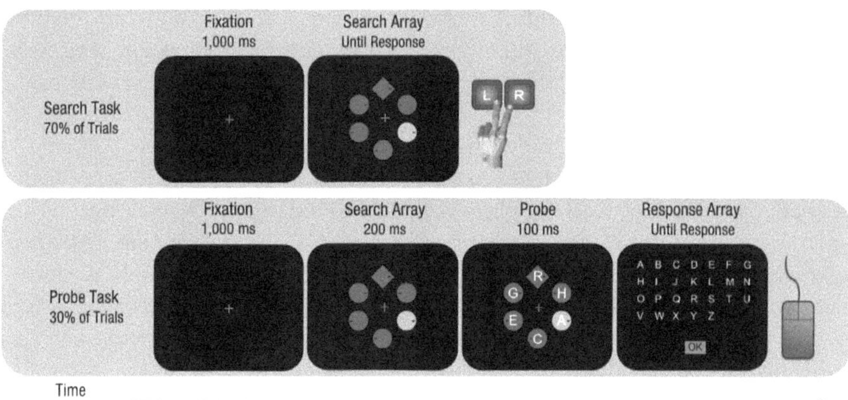

Figure 4.2 An illustration of the capture-probe paradigm. On search trials (upper panel), participants search for the target (diamond). On probe trials, they report the probe letters they could identify. A distractor (here, the light grey circle) is either present or absent.
Source: reproduced with permission from Gaspelin et al. (2015)

diamond) among nontargets sharing the target's color (e.g., green) and one distractor which, when present, has a unique color (e.g., red). The salient distractor is said to capture attention if performance is slower when it is present vs. absent, and to be suppressed if the opposite result is obtained. On a minority of (probe) trials, shortly after the search display appears, a letter is presented briefly at each object's location and masked; participants report the letters they were able to identify. The salient distractor is said to capture attention if participants report more probes from the salient distractor's location than from the average nontarget's location.

Wang and Theeuwes (2020) manipulated the irrelevant-color distractor's salience and found the signature of attentional suppression when the distractor was less salient and the signature of attentional capture when the distractor was more salient. They concluded that only salience guides attention and denied any role for feature-based suppression—although they did not manipulate feature-based suppression. Stilwell and Gaspelin (2021) reported the signature of feature-based suppression on both measures with highly salient distractors and concluded that feature-based suppression overrides stimulus salience—but manipulated neither stimulus salience nor feature-based suppression. The most parsimonious account for these findings is that both salience and feature-based suppression modulate priority weights, with the net outcome of these opposing forces (e.g., a benefit or a cost of a salient distractor's presence) depending on the idiosyncratic conditions prevailing in the experiment—a conclusion that we confirmed by jointly manipulating both sources of attentional guidance (Ramgir & Lamy, 2023).

The common problem that this example illustrates is that many of the lingering divergences in attentional guidance research are rooted in the fact that the authors often base their conclusions on net capture/suppression effects rather than on the modulation of these effects by relevant variables, and thereby conflate effects with mechanisms (Lamy, 2021).

3.2.2 Redefining attentional capture

What attentional capture refers to is straightforward: it occurs when we direct our attention to a stimulus in contradiction with our momentary goals. A high-contrast stimulus (e.g., a color singleton), a "special" stimulus (e.g., an abrupt onset or an angry face) or a stimulus with a attended or rewarded feature captures our attention if we shift our attention to its location rather than to the target. However, it is important to recognize that this is not what the main paradigms used to study attentional capture actually measure (e.g., the additional singleton and capture-probe paradigms described in the previous section; see also the spatial-cueing paradigm discussed in section 4). For instance, distractor interference (slower performance when the distractor is present vs. absent) in the additional-singleton paradigm, probably the most popular measure of attentional capture, only indexes that this stimulus has higher priority than the nontarget that it replaces: the classical finding that in search for a green diamond among green circles (Figure 4.3a), performance is slower when one green circle is replaced with a red circle (Figure 4.3b), only indicates that

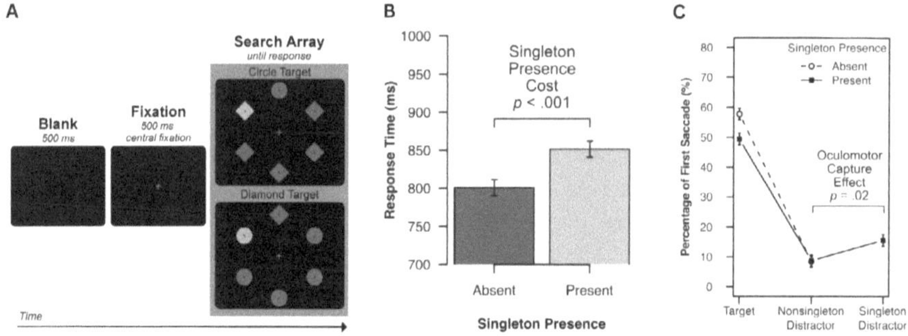

Figure 4.3 (a) Typical search display in the additional-singleton paradigm. (b) The presence of the color-singleton distractor interferes with search, but (c) the proportion of first saccades by object type (target, singleton distractor, nonsingleton distractors) clearly indicates that the target benefits from higher attentional priority than the singleton distractor.

Source: reproduced with permission from Gaspelin et al. (2017)

the red circle competes more strongly with the target than the green circle (Wirth, Ramgir & Lamy, 2023).

Evidence for our claim clearly emerges from the pattern of results observed in this task with measures that directly probe where attention is allocated. Consider Figure 4.3c, which shows the percentage of first saccades that landed on a given stimulus type (target, nontarget, or distractor): it is clear, that although distractor interference was substantial (Figure 4.3b), most first saccades landed on the target. The distractor (red circle) only prevailed relative to nontargets (green circles), not relative to the target. These findings indicate that attentional capture occurs because selectivity is not perfect: even when attention is strongly guided by the known target feature (here, the diamond), it sometimes lands at an irrelevant location, which occurs more often the higher the priority weight at that location.

To summarize our argument, finding that the presence of a critical distractor interferes with search does not entail that this distractor overrides search goals. What pattern of results, then, would be required to conclude that a given type of stimulus is "special" in its ability to capture attention, rather than simply intrinsically endowed with a larger priority weight than another stimulus type (e.g., angry faces relative to neutral faces)? It seems reasonable to require that special stimuli, if they exist, should be objects that receive the first shift of attention or the first eye saccade *most often* (i.e., more often than the target) in a large variety of task contexts.

3.2.3 The role of habituation and learned suppression

The idea that attentional capture should occur so rarely contradicts our subjective daily experience: anyone would agree that the sudden noise of a slamming door would reflexively capture their attention in almost any situation. Reviving early work on the effect of repeated exposure to an irrelevant stimulus on the orienting response (i.e., habituation; Sokolov, 1963), more recent research suggests a simple answer to this apparent contradiction: certain categories of stimuli may have the intrinsic ability to capture attention automatically, but we learn to ignore them after a few exposures, when they are task-irrelevant and have no consequences requiring our consideration: if the door slams repeatedly because of the wind, one will quickly stop paying attention to it and may eventually fail to even notice the noise.

Several studies supported this idea (e.g., Folk & Remington, 2015; Turatto & Pascucci, 2016; Vatterott & Vecera, 2012). For instance, Vatterott and Vecera (2012) introduced a twist in the additional singleton paradigm by changing the color of the unique distractor on each block of trials. They found that the presence of the distractor impaired search during the first half of each block but not during the second half. They concluded that a distractor can be ignored through learned suppression of its salient feature.

Note that based on the argument developed in section 3.2.2, this finding demonstrates that an irrelevant object's priority decreases after a few exposures. However, it does not necessarily entail that early on, this object was more likely than *any* other object to receive attention (i.e., that it captured attention). To answer this question, it would be useful to investigate the effect of just a few exposures to candidate "special" stimuli (and ideally, just one, e.g., Gibson & Jiang, 1998), using direct measures of attentional allocation (e.g., first saccades or probe reports).

To summarize, there is currently no convincing evidence that one source of guidance has an intrinsic advantage over the others, or that certain classes of stimuli are special in their ability to summon attention automatically or interrupt current behavior. Here, we argued that current claims to the contrary rely on misinterpretations of the measures held to index attentional capture. Indeed, the impact of a given source of guidance has often been overestimated because the simple finding that it influences attentional priority has been misconstrued as evidence that it elicits automatic attentional capture. However, the potential ability of some special stimuli to summon attention by vetoing other sources of guidance may also have been underestimated because the impact of these stimuli on performance is typically gauged across an entire experiment. Given mounting evidence suggesting that an irrelevant object's attentional priority decreases after just a few exposures, it will be important to measure actual shifts of attention to these objects rather than their indirect impact on performance, very early in practice.

4 The missing ingredient: temporal attention

4.1 Similarities between spatial and temporal attention

A largely separate body of research has shown that attention can be directed not only to space, but also to relevant points in time (see Nobre, Nobre & Coull, 2010 for a review). For instance, a tennis player will focus her attention at the location where she prepares to hit the ball, at the exact moment when she expects it to arrive there. If she deploys her attention too late, she will most likely miss the ball.

Interestingly, similar phenomena were discovered for temporal and for spatial attention. A cue indicating *where* a target is likely to appear speeds performance and so does a cue indicating *when* it is likely to appear (e.g., Coull & Nobre, 1998). Statistical regularities as to *where* a target will appear speed search and so do statistical regularities as to *when* within a sequence of events a target will appear (e.g., Yashar & Lamy, 2013). A random repetition of the target *location* on successive trials speeds search (Maljkovic & Nakayama, 1996), and so does a random repetition of *when* the target appears (Yashar & Lamy, 2013).

Despite these similarities, there has been no systematic effort to integrate the mechanisms underlying attentional prioritization of individual features, feature dimensions and locations and the mechanisms underlying attentional prioritization of moments in time into one general model. In particular, the temporal dimension of attention is conspicuously absent from the priority map on which recent models of attention converge (e.g., Anderson et al., 2021; Luck et al., 2021; Todd & Manaligod, 2018; Wolfe, 2021). In fact, these models implicitly deny any role for temporal attention. Specifically, considering that our environment, experience and goals are dynamic, these models typically assume that the priority weights on the priority map change constantly and that the focus of our attention is yoked to the location of the highest-priority object. For instance, Bisley and Mirpour (2019) suggested that "unlike overt attention (i.e., gaze), covert attention is allocated to the peak of a priority map on a moment-by-moment basis" (p. 110). However, if we can attend to specific points in time, a time-related mechanism must gate the reading out of the priority map that leads to attentional allocation. In other words, if at any given moment the peak of activation on the priority map *is* the focus of our attention, it is not clear how temporal information can influence whether attention will be deployed at one moment or at another.

4.2 *Do cue validity effects index attentional capture?*

The standard interpretation of cue validity effects provides a telling illustration of this widespread *online-prioritization* assumption. Cue validity effects are measured using the spatial cueing paradigm (Folk, Remington & Johnston, 1992). In a typical experiment, participants search for a target among distractors and a non-informative cue appears at one potential target location, shortly before the search display (Figure 4.4). For instance, the cue may be an abrupt-onset object, which participants must ignore. Finding that search performance is faster when the target appears at the same location as the cue location (valid-cue trials) than elsewhere (invalid-cue trials) is taken as evidence that the cue captured attention because it was the highest-priority object on the screen when the cueing display appeared.

Note that participants could in principle take advantage of the temporal regularities embedded in the task to deploy their attention at the appropriate moment and avoid attentional capture by the cue: the target always appears in

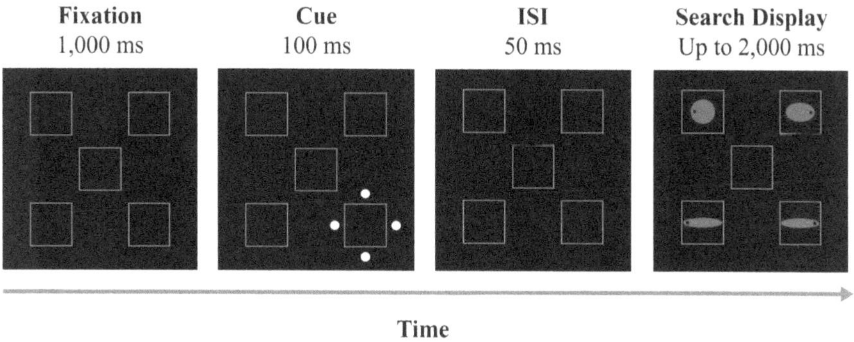

Figure 4.4 Typical spatial cueing paradigm. Participants search for the target (circle). The cue (the four abruptly onset dots) is not informative as to where the target will appear.

the search display (never in the cue display), and typically at a fixed time. Given the importance of temporal attention for survival in a dynamic environment and the many demonstrations that it can guide our attention (e.g., Nobre et al., 2010) with exquisite temporal resolution (e.g., Lamy, 2005), why do involuntary shifts of attention occur in the spatial-cueing paradigm?

We recently challenged the widespread idea that cue validity effects index actual shifts of attention (Lamy et al., 2018). In doing so, we were motivated by a number of puzzling findings (see Darnell & Lamy, 2022 for a detailed discussion). For example, an abrupt-onset cue produces a large cue-validity effect when the search is difficult (e.g., when target-distractor similarity is high) but yields no effect whatsoever when the search is easy, even when easy and difficult-search trials are randomly mixed (e.g., Darnell & Lamy, 2022; Gaspelin et al., 2016). How could characteristics of the search display affect whether or not a cue on a preceding display captures attention? To explain this counter-intuitive finding, Gaspelin et al. (2016; Ruthruff et al., 2020) proposed the attentional dwelling hypothesis: the cue captures attention during both easy and difficult search but attention is rapidly disengaged from the cued distractor when this distractor is easy to reject and dwells there longer when the cued distractor is difficult to reject. That attention should dwell longer on a distractor's location the more similar this distractor is to the target is a reasonable hypothesis. However, how can attention be disengaged from an object and moved across a distance of 10° of visual angle in no time at all? This assumption is difficult to reconcile with what is known about how fast attention moves in space (e.g., Tsal, 1983).

4.3 The Priority Accumulation Framework

To account for these and other findings (see Darnell & Lamy, 2022 for review), we recently suggested a new conceptual framework to think about attentional allocation, the Priority Accumulation Framework (PAF; Lamy et al., 2018). The main difference between PAF and current models of attention concerns how dynamic changes on the priority map affect the allocation of attention (Figure 4.5). According

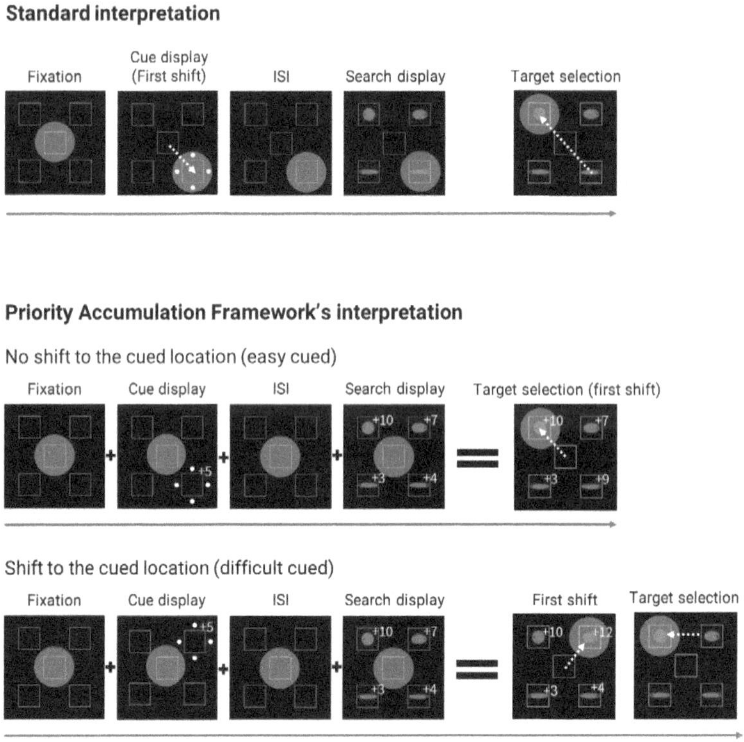

Figure 4.5 Competing interpretations of spatial cueing effects. Standard interpretation (upper row): attention was shifted to the cue and remained at its location until the search display appeared. Priority Accumulation Framework interpretation (lower rows): attentional priority accumulates across time and attention is shifted to the location with the highest accumulated priority after the search display appears, with cue-validity effects indicating that the cue biased the competition.

Source: reproduced with permission from Darnell and Lamy (2021)

to PAF, priority weights accumulate over time at each location, until information associated with the appearance of the target (henceforth, temporal or contextual information) signals that selection can occur. The first attentional shift is then made to the item that wins the competition (i.e., at the location with the highest accumulated priority). Because the control of temporal or contextual information on selection is not perfect, selection sometimes occurs at the wrong moment.

This framework can account for many previous findings. For instance, it explains why attentional capture by an onset cue depends on search difficulty. During easy search, the target's edge over the distractors is so large that the addition of the onset cue's activation (on valid vs. invalid trials) has a negligible impact on the probability that the target will win the competition and how fast. By contrast, during difficult search, where the competition is strong, this impact is substantial.

In addition, PAF yields testable predictions, several of which were recently supported (e.g., Darnell & Lamy, 2022; Toledano et al., 2024; Yaron & Lamy, 2021; Gabbay et al., 2019). For instance, Toledano et al. (2024) measured eye movements, while participants performed a search task and moved their eyes freely – a situation where eye saccades are closely coupled to shifts of attention (e.g., Findlay, 2005). Distractors were either similar to the target (difficult search) or dissimilar to it (easy search). According to PAF, most first saccades should be initiated after the search display appears; more of these late saccades should land on the cued vs. uncued distractor locations, and, crucially, the advantage at the cue location should increase the more difficult the search. All these predictions were confirmed.

According to models assuming that attention is automatically directed to the highest-priority object "online," the proportion of first saccades to the cued location should not depend on search difficulty because they occur in response to the cue display.

To summarize, we illustrated the need to integrate the insights that previous research on spatial and temporal attention have generated in largely separate lines of research. Our main message is that an important task for future research is to provide a mechanistic account of how temporal attention interacts with the priority map to determine how we allocate our attention in a dynamic world. The PAF, although still tentative, is a small step in this direction.

5 Conclusions and directions for future research

Research over the last decade or so has vastly improved our understanding of the factors that determine where we will shift our attention next. In this research, the concept of a priority map has played a prominent role, as most current models of attention posit the existence of a dynamic representation that integrates several sources of information to rank the locations in our visual field by order of importance, and thereby ensures that we prioritize the most relevant events for immediate action. A major development in this field that has partly defused enduring controversies, is the realization that, in addition to salient events and objects matching our explicit goals, our past experience has powerful and long-lasting effects on our search behavior. Here, we suggested that two main aspects of this research impede its progress. The first is that researchers in the field still expend considerable effort in order to demonstrate that one source of guidance overrides another, and fail to acknowledge that the relative contributions of different sources of guidance are most probably idiosyncratic to specific experimental conditions. The second is that current research on spatial and on temporal attention remains largely separate, even though it is impossible to understand how we prioritize information in an ever-changing environment without elucidating how spatial and temporal attention interact. Addressing these two issues is a major goal for future investigations of how we dynamically allocate our attention to optimize performance.

Note

1 Several authors have also suggested that attentional guidance also depends on the required motor action (e.g., Cisek & Kalaska, 2010).

References

Arita, J. T., Carlisle, N. B. & Woodman, G. F. (2012). Templates for rejection: Configuring attention to ignore task-irrelevant features. *Journal of Experimental Psychology: Human Perception and Performance*, 38(3), 580–584. https://doi.org/10.1037/a0027885.

Awh, E., Belopolsky, A. V. & Theeuwes, J. (2012). Top-down versus bottom-up attentional control: A failed theoretical dichotomy. *Trends in Cognitive Sciences*, 16(8), 437–443. https://doi.org/10.1016/j.tics.2012.06.010.

Anderson, B. A. (2019). Neurobiology of value-driven attention. *Current Opinion in Psychology*, 29, 27–33. https://doi.org/10.1016/j.copsyc.2018.11.004.

Anderson, B. A., Kim, H., Kim, A. J., Liao, M. R., Mrkonja, L., Clement, A. & Grégoire, L. (2021). The past, present, and future of selection history. *Neuroscience & Biobehavioral Reviews*, 130, 326–350. https://doi.org/10.1016/j.neubiorev.2021.09.004.

Anderson, B. A., Laurent, P. A. & Yantis, S. (2011). Value-driven attentional capture. *Proceedings of the National Academy of Sciences*, 108(25), 10367–10371. https://doi.org/10.1073/pnas.1104047108.

Bacon, W. F. & Egeth, H. E. (1994). Overriding stimulus-driven attentional capture. *Perception & Psychophysics*, 55(5), 485–496. https://doi.org/10.3758/BF03205306.

Beck, V. M., Hollingworth, A. & Luck, S. J. (2012). Simultaneous control of attention by multiple working memory representations. *Psychological Science*, 23(8), 887–898.

Belopolsky, A. V., Schreij, D. & Theeuwes, J. (2010). What is top-down about contingent capture? *Attention, Perception & Psychophysics*, 72, 326–341. https://doi.org/10.3758/APP.72.2.326.

Bisley, J. W. & Mirpour, K. (2019). The neural instantiation of a priority map. *Current opinion in psychology*, 29, 108–112. https://doi.org/10.1016/j.copsyc.2019.01.002.

Broadbent, D. E. (1958). *Perception and communication*. Pergamon Press.

Cave, K. R. & Wolfe, J. M. (1990). Modeling the role of parallel processing in visual search. *Cognitive Psychology, 22*(2), 225–271. https://doi.org/10.1016/0010-0285(90)90017-X.

Chun, M. M. & Jiang, Y. (1998). Contextual cueing: Implicit learning and memory of visual context guides spatial attention. *Cognitive Psychology*, 36(1), 28–71. https://doi.org/10.1006/cogp.1998.0681.

Cisek, P. & Kalaska, J. F. (2010). Neural mechanisms for interacting with a world full of action choices. *Annual Review of Neuroscience*, 33(1), 269–298. https://doi.org./10.1146/annurev.neuro.051508.135409.

Cochrane, B. A. & Pratt, J. (2020). Re-examining Maljkovic and Nakayama (1994): Conscious expectancy does affect the Priming of Pop-out effect. *Attention, Perception & Psychophysics* 82(5), 2693–2702. https://doi.org/10.3758/s13414-020-02034-x.

Coull, J. T. & Nobre, A. C. (1998). Where and when to pay attention: the neural systems for directing attention to spatial locations and to time intervals as revealed by both PET and fMRI. *Journal of Neuroscience*, 18(18), 7426–7435. https://doi.org/10.1523/JNEUROSCI.18-18-07426.1998.

Darnell, M. & Lamy, D. (2022). Spatial cueing effects do not always index attentional capture: Evidence for a Priority Accumulation Framework. *Psychological Research*, 86 (5), 1547–1564. https://doi.org/10.1007/s00426-021-01597-0.

Desimone, R. & Duncan, J. (1995). Neural mechanisms of selective visual attention. *Annual Review of Neuroscience*, 18(1), 193–222.

Egeth, H. (2018). Comment on Theeuwes's characterization of visual selection. *Journal of Cognition*, 1(1).

Egeth, H. E. & Yantis, S. (1997). Visual attention: Control, representation, and time course. *Annual Review of Psychology*, 48(1), 269–297.

Eriksen, C. W. & St James, J. D. (1986). Visual attention within and around the field of focal attention: A zoom lens model. *Perception & Psychophysics*, 40(4), 225–240. https://doi.org/10.3758/BF03211502.

Ferrante, O., Patacca, A., Di Caro, V., Della Libera, C., Santandrea, E. & Chelazzi, L. (2018). Altering spatial priority maps via statistical learning of target selection and distractor filtering. *Cortex*, 102, 67–95. https://doi.org/10.1016/j.cortex.2017.09.027.

Findlay, J. M. (2005). Covert attention and saccadic eye movements. In L. Itti, G. Rees & J. K. Tsotsos (Eds.), *Neurobiology of attention* (pp. 114–116). Academic Press. https://doi.org/10.1016/B978-012375731-9/50024-0.

Folk, C. L., Leber, A. B. & Egeth, H. E. (2002). Made you blink! Contingent attentional capture produces a spatial blink. *Perception & Psychophysics*, 64(5), 741–753. https://doi.org/10.3758/BF03194741.

Folk, C. L. & Remington, R. W. (2015). Unexpected abrupt onsets can override a top-down set for color. *Journal of Experimental Psychology: Human Perception and Performance*, 41(4), 1153. https://doi.org/10.1037/xhp0000084.

Folk, C. L., Remington, R. W. & Johnston, J. C. (1992). Involuntary covert orienting is contingent on attentional control settings. *Journal of Experimental Psychology: Human Perception and Performance*, 18(4), 1030. https://doi.org/10.1037/0096-1523.18.4.1030.

Found, A. & Müller, H. J. (1996). Searching for unknown feature targets on more than one dimension: Investigating a "dimension-weighting" account. *Perception & Psychophysics*, 58(1), 88–101. https://doi.org/10.3758/BF03205479.

Gabbay, C., Zivony, A. & Lamy, D. (2019). Splitting the attentional spotlight? Evidence from attentional capture by successive events. *Visual Cognition*, 27(5–8), 518–536. https://doi.org/10.1080/13506285.2019.1617377.

Gaspelin, N., Leonard, C. J. & Luck, S. J. (2015). Direct evidence for active suppression of salient-but-irrelevant sensory inputs. *Psychological Science, 26*(11), 1740–1750. https://doi.org/10.1177/0956797615597913.

Gaspelin, N., Leonard, C. J. & Luck, S. J. (2017). Suppression of overt attentional capture by salient-but-irrelevant color singletons. *Attention, Perception, & Psychophysics*, 79, 45–62.

Gaspelin, N., Ruthruff, E. & Lien, M. C. (2016). The problem of latent attentional capture: Easy visual search conceals capture by task-irrelevant abrupt onsets. *Journal of Experimental Psychology: Human Perception and Performance*, 42(8), 1104–1120. https://doi.org/10.1037/xhp0000214.

Gazzaniga, M. S., Heatherton, T. F. & Halpern, D. (2016). *Psychological Science*, 5th edition. W. W. Norton and Company.

Geng, J. J. & Behrmann, M. (2005). Spatial probability as an attentional cue in visual search. *Perception & psychophysics*, 67(7), 1252–1268. https://doi.org/10.3758/BF03193557.

Gibson, B. S. & Jiang, Y. (1998). Surprise! An unexpected color singleton does not capture attention in visual search. *Psychological science*, 9(3), 176–182. https://doi.org/10.1111/1467-9280.0003.

Giménez-Fernández, T., Luque, D., Shanks, D. R. & Vadillo, M. A. (2023). Rethinking attentional habits. *Current Directions in Psychological Science*, 32(6), 494–500. https://doi.org/10.1177/09637214231191976.

Golan, A. & Lamy, D. (2022a). Is statistical learning of a salient distractor's color implicit, inflexible and distinct from inter-trial priming? *Journal of Cognition*, 5(1), 47. http://doi.org/10.5334/joc.243.

Golan, A. & Lamy, D. (2022b). Out of control: Attentional guidance by statistical learning of target location. *Journal of Vision*, 22(14), 3554.

Gottlieb, J. P., Kusunoki, M. & Goldberg, M. E. (1998). The representation of visual salience in monkey parietal cortex. *Nature*, 391(6666), 481–484. https://doi.org/10.1038/35135.

Jiang, Y. V. (2018). Habitual versus goal-driven attention. *Cortex*, 102, 107–120.

Knudsen, E. I. (2007). Fundamental components of attention. *Annual review of neuroscience* 30, 57–78.

Koch, C. & Ullman, S. (1985). Shifts in selective visual attention: towards the underlying neural circuitry. *Human Neurobiology*, 4(4), 219–227.

Kustov, A. A. & Lee Robinson, D. (1996). Shared neural control of attentional shifts and eye movements. *Nature*, 384(6604), 74–77. https://doi.org/10.1038/384074a0.

Lamy, D. (2005). Temporal expectations modulate attentional capture. *Psychonomic Bulletin & Review*, 12(6), 1112–1119. https://doi.org/10.3758/BF03206452.

Lamy, D. (2021). The attentional capture debate: The long-lasting consequences of a misnomer. *Visual Cognition*, 29(9), 544–547. https://doi.org/10.1080/13506285.2021.1904076.

Lamy, D., Antebi, C., Aviani, N. & Carmel, T. (2008a). Priming of pop-out provides reliable measures of target activation and distractor inhibition in selective attention. *Vision research*, 48(1), 30–41. https://doi.org/10.1016/j.visres.2007.10.009.

Lamy, D., Bar-Anan, Y. & Egeth, H. E. (2008b). The role of within-dimension singleton priming in visual search. *Journal of Experimental Psychology: Human Perception and Performance*, 34(2), 268–285. https://doi.org/10.1037/0096-1523.34.2.268.

Lamy, D., Amunts, L. & Bar-Haim, Y. (2008c). Emotional priming of pop-out in visual search. *Emotion*, 8(2), 151–161. https://doi.org/10.1037/1528-3542.8.2.151.

Lamy, D., Darnell, M., Levi, A. & Bublil, C. (2018). Testing the attentional dwelling hypothesis of attentional capture. *Journal of Cognition*, 1(1), 1–16. http://doi.org/10.5334/joc.48.

Lamy, D., Leber, A. & Egeth, H. E. (2004). Effects of task relevance and stimulus-driven salience in feature-search mode. *Journal of Experimental Psychology: Human Perception and Performance*, 30(6), 1019–1031. https://doi.org/10.1037/0096-1523.30.6.1019..

Lamy, D. F. & Kristjánsson, Á. (2013). Is goal-directed attentional guidance just intertrial priming? A review. *Journal of Vision*, 13(3), 14–14. https://doi.org/10.1167/13.3.14.

Lamy, D. & Tsal, Y. (2000). Object features, object locations, and object files: Which does selective attention activate and when?. *Journal of Experimental Psychology: Human Perception and Performance*, 26(4), 1387–1400. https://doi.org/10.1037/0096-1523.26.4.1387..

Liesefeld, H. R., Lamy, D. et al. (2024). Terms of debate: Consensus definitions to guide the scientific discourse on visual distraction. *Attention, Perception and Psychophysics*, 1–28. https://doi.org/10.3758/s13414-023-02820-3.

Luck, S. J., Gaspelin, N., Folk, C. L., Remington, R. W. & Theeuwes, J. (2021). Progress toward resolving the attentional capture debate. *Visual Cognition*, 29(1), 1–21. https://doi.org/10.1080/13506285.2020.1848949.

Maljkovic, V. & Nakayama, K. (1994). Priming of pop-out: I. Role of features. *Memory & cognition*, 22(6), 657–672. https://doi.org/10.3758/BF03209251.

Maljkovic, V. & Nakayama, K. E. N. (1996). Priming of pop-out: II. The role of position. *Perception & Psychophysics*, 58(7), 977–991. https://doi.org/10.3758/BF03206826.

Müller, H. J. & Rabbitt, P. M. (1989). Reflexive and voluntary orienting of visual attention: time course of activation and resistance to interruption. *Journal of Experimental Psychology: Human Perception and Performance*, 15(2), 315–330. https://doi.org/10.1037/0096-1523.15.2.315.

Navalpakkam, V. & Itti, L. (2005). Modeling the influence of task on attention. *Vision research*, 45(2), 205–231. https://doi.org/10.1016/j.visres.2004.07.042.

Neisser, U. (1967). *Cognitive psychology*. Appleton, Century, Crofts.

Nobre, A. C., Nobre, K. & Coull, J. T. (Eds.). (2010). *Attention and time*. Oxford University Press.

Pearson, D., Donkin, C., Tran, S. C., Most, S. B. & Le Pelley, M. E. (2015). Cognitive control and counterproductive oculomotor capture by reward-related stimuli. *Visual Cognition*, 23(1–2), 41–66. https://doi.org/10.1080/13506285.2014.994252.

Pearson, D., Watson, P., Cheng, P. X. & Le Pelley, M. E. (2020). Overt attentional capture by reward-related stimuli overcomes inhibitory suppression. *Journal of Experimental Psychology: Human Perception and Performance*, 46(5), 489–501. https://doi.org/10.1037/xhp0000728.

Posner, M. I. (1980). Orienting of attention. *Quarterly Journal of Experimental Psychology*, 32(1), 3–25.

Posner, M. I. & Cohen, Y. (1984). *Components of attention*. In H. Bouma & D. G. Bouwhuis (Eds.), *Attention and performance* X (pp. 55–66). Erlbaum.

Ramgir, A. & Lamy, D. (2021). Does feature intertrial priming guide attention? The jury is still out. *Psychonomic Bulletin & Review*, 1–25. https://doi.org/10.3758/s13423-021-01997-8.

Ramgir, A. & Lamy, D. (2023). Distractor's salience does not determine feature suppression: A commentary on Wang and Theeuwes (2020). *Journal of Experimental Psychology: Human Perception and Performance*, 49(6), 852–861. https://doi.org/10.1037/xhp0001119.

Ruthruff, E., Faulks, M., Maxwell, J. W. & Gaspelin, N. (2020). Attentional dwelling and capture by color singletons. *Attention, Perception & Psychophysics*, 82(6), 3048–3064. https://doi.org/10.3758/s13414-020-02054-7.

Serences, J. T. & Kastner, S. (2014). A multi-level account of selective attention. In A. C. Nobre & S. Kastner (Eds.), *The Oxford handbook of attention* (pp. 76–104). Oxford University Press.

Sokolov, E. N. (1963). Higher nervous functions; the orienting reflex. *Annual Review of Physiology*, 25, 545–580. http://dx.doi.org/10.1146/annurev.ph.25.030163.002553.

Sprague, T. C., Itthipuripat, S., Vo, V. A. & Serences, J. T. (2018). Dissociable signatures of visual salience and behavioral relevance across attentional priority maps in human cortex. *Journal of Neurophysiology*, 119(6), 2153–2165. https://doi.org/10.1152/jn.00059.2018.

Stilwell, B. T., Bahle, B. & Vecera, S. P. (2019). Feature-based statistical regularities of distractors modulate attentional capture. *Journal of Experimental Psychology: Human Perception and Performance*, 45(3), 419–433. https://doi.org/10.1037/xhp0000613.

Stilwell, B. T. & Gaspelin, N. (2021). Attentional suppression of highly salient color singletons. *Journal of Experimental Psychology: Human Perception and Performance*, 47(10), 1313–1328. https://doi.org/10.1037/xhp0000948.

Theeuwes, J. (1991). Cross-dimensional perceptual selectivity. *Perception & Psychophysics*, 50 (2). https://doi.org/10.3758/BF03212219.

Theeuwes, J. (2004). Top-down search strategies cannot override attentional capture. *Psychonomic Bulletin & Review*, 11(1), 65–70. https://doi.org/10.3758/BF03206462.

Theeuwes, J. (2010). Top–down and bottom–up control of visual selection. *Acta psychologica*, 135(2), 77–99. https://doi.org/10.1016/j.actpsy.2010.02.006.

Theeuwes, J. (2018). Visual selection: Usually fast and automatic; seldom slow and volitional. *Journal of Cognition*, 1(1), article 29. https://doi.org/10.5334/joc.13.

Thompson, K. G., Bichot, N. P. & Schall, J. D. (1997). Dissociation of visual discrimination from saccade programming in macaque frontal eye field. *Journal of Neurophysiology*, 77(2), 1046–1050. https://doi.org/10.1152/jn.1997.77.2.1046.

Todd, R. M. & Manaligod, M. G. (2018). Implicit guidance of attention: The priority state space framework. *Cortex*, 102, 121–138. https://doi.org/10.1016/j.cortex.2017.08.001.

Toledano, D. & Lamy, D., (In press). Priming of location (PoL) revisited: reanalysis of a large-scale database. *Visual Cognition*.

Toledano, D., Sasi, M., Yuval-Greenberg, S. & Lamy, D. (2024). On the timing of overt attention deployment: Eye-movement evidence for the priority accumulation framework. *Journal of Experimental Psychology: Human Perception and Performance*, 50 (5), 431–450. https://doi.org/10.1037/xhp0001192.

Torralba, A., Oliva, A., Castelhano, M. S. & Henderson, J. M. (2006). Contextual guidance of eye movements and attention in real-world scenes: the role of global features in object search. *Psychological Review*, 113(4), 766–786. https://doi.org/10.1037/0033-295X.113.4.766.

Treisman, A. & Gelade, G. (1980). A feature-integration theory of attention. Cog*nitive Psychology*, 12, 97–136. https://doi.org/10.1016/0010-0285(80)90005-5.

Tsal, Y. (1983). Movement of attention across the visual field. *Journal of Experimental Psychology: Human Perception and Performance*, 9(4), 523–530. https://doi.org/10.1037/0096-1523.9.4.523.

Turatto, M. & Pascucci, D. (2016). Short-term and long-term plasticity in the visual-attention system: Evidence from habituation of attentional capture. *Neurobiology of Learning and Memory*, 130, 159–169. https://doi.org/10.1016/j.nlm.2016.02.010.

Vadillo, M. A., Linssen, D., Orgaz, C., Parsons, S. & Shanks, D. R. (2020). Unconscious or underpowered? Probabilistic cuing of visual attention. *Journal of Experimental Psychology: General*, 149(1), 160–181. https://doi.org/10.1037/xge0000632.

van Heusden, E., van Zoest, W., Donk, M. & Olivers, C. N. (2022). An attentional limbo: Saccades become momentarily non-selective in between saliency-driven and relevance-driven selection. *Psychonomic Bulletin & Review*, 29, 1327–1337 (2022). https://doi.org/10.3758/s13423-022-02091-3.

van Zoest, W., Donk, M. & Theeuwes, J. (2004). The role of stimulus-driven and goal-driven control in saccadic visual selection. *Journal of Experimental Psychology: Human Perception and Performance*, 30(4), 746–759. https://doi.org/10.1037/0096-1523.30.4.749.

Vatterott, D. B. & Vecera, S. P. (2012). Experience-dependent attentional tuning of distractor rejection. *Psychonomic Bulletin & Review*, 19(5), 871–878. https://doi.org/10.3758/s13423-012-0280-4.

Wang, B. & Theeuwes, J. (2018). Statistical regularities modulate attentional capture. *Journal of Experimental Psychology: Human Perception and Performance*, 44(1), 13–17. https://doi.org/10.1037/xhp0000472.

Wang, B. & Theeuwes, J. (2020). Salience determines attentional orienting in visual selection. *Journal of Experimental Psychology: Human Perception and Performance*, 46(10), 1051–1057. https://doi.org/10.1037/xhp0000796.

White, B. J., Kan, J. Y., Levy, R., Itti, L. & Munoz, D. P. (2017). Superior colliculus encodes visual saliency before the primary visual cortex. *Proceedings of the National Academy of Sciences*, 114(35), 9451–9456. https://doi.org/10.1073/pnas.170100311.

Wirth, B. E., Ramgir, A. & Lamy, D. (2023). Feature intertrial priming biases attentional priority: Evidence from the capture-probe paradigm. *Journal of Experimental Psychology: Human Perception and Performance*, 49(8), 1145–1157. https://doi.org/10.1037/xhp0001135.

Wolfe, J. M. (2021). Guided Search 6.0: An updated model of visual search. *Psychonomic Bulletin & Review*, 28(4), 1060–1092. https://doi.org/10.3758/s13423-020-01859-9.

Wolfe, J. M., Cave, K. R. & Franzel, S. L. (1989). Guided search: An alternative to the Feature Integration model for visual search. *Journal of Experimental Psychology: Human Perception and Performance*, 15, 419–433. https://doi.org/10.1037/0096-1523.15.3.419.

Yantis, S. & Jones, E. (1991). Mechanisms of attentional selection: Temporally modulated priority tags. *Perception & Psychophysics*, 50(2), 166–178. https://doi.org/10.3758/BF03212217.

Yantis, S. & Jonides, J. (1990). Abrupt visual onsets and selective attention: voluntary versus automatic allocation. *Journal of Experimental Psychology: Human Perception and Performance*, 16(1), 121. https://doi.org/10.1037/0096-1523.16.1.121.

Yaron, I. & Lamy, D. (2021). Spatial cueing effects are not what we thought: On the timing of attentional deployment. *Journal of Experimental Psychology: Human Perception and Performance*, 47(7), 946–962. https://doi.org/10.1037/xhp0000918.

Yashar, A. & Lamy, D. (2013). Temporal position priming: Memory traces of recent experience bias the allocation of attention in time. *Journal of Experimental Psychology: Human Perception and Performance*, 39(5), 1443–1456. https://doi.org/10.1037/a0031231.

Zelinsky, G. J. & Bisley, J. W. (2015). The what, where, and why of priority maps and their interactions with visual working memory. *Annals of the New York Academy of Sciences*, 1339(1), 154–164. https://doi.org/10.1111/nyas.12606.

5 Role of consciousness in distractor avoidance

Vaishnavi Mohite, Seema Prasad and Ramesh Kumar Mishra

1 What is distractor suppression?

While walking in a park we notice an array of trees, flowers and other human beings. What we might fail to notice is the shape of the leaves, the size of the petals and facial expressions of those we pass by. When attention is not focused on something, a gist of perception gives us the information we need. Interestingly, even in this diffused state, our eyes are more likely to fall on the newer leaves, fresh flowers and people wearing flashy clothes or with unusual appearances. This happens because these elements in the surrounding may stand out in color, brightness, luminance, contrast and other visual features, and such inconsistencies capture attention (Folk, Remington & Wright, 1994). Studies using visual search tasks, which are typically used to measure the influence of distractors on search behavior, show that a brightly colored (salient) distractor often captures attention before attention is directed to the target of the search. In the absence of a salient distractor, attention can be directed directly to the target (Liesefeld, Liesefeld, Töllner & Müller, 2017; Theeuwes, 1992). Hence, filtering of distractors is necessary to utilize attentional resources effectively (Broadbent, 1982, 2013). This chapter will deal with the issue of how distractors are avoided and whether this can be achieved unconsciously. We first review the concept of distractor suppression and describe the current models that attempt to explain the mechanism underlying distractor suppression. Next, we discuss if there is a theoretical basis to expect that distractor suppression can proceed in the absence of conscious awareness and examine existing evidence in favor of this hypothesis. We conclude the chapter by suggesting directions of future research.

Selection of a "target" is only the final outcome of filtering distractors from the visual field but the mechanism leading to it is far more complicated than previously assumed (Failing, Wang & Theeuwes, 2019; Geng, 2014). Selection has traditionally been viewed as a unitary mechanism which compares all items to *target representations* and enhances attentional processing of matching items (target enhancement), discard mismatching items and keeps them out of the attentional focus (Bichot, Rossi & Desimone, 2005; Findlay, 1997). Recently an additional mechanism called *distractor suppression* has been discovered which uniquely inhibits distractors that have the capacity to capture attention more

DOI: 10.4324/9781003360896-5

strongly than other distractors (Hickey, Di Lollo & McDonald, 2009; Schneider, Herbst, Klatt & Wöstmann, 2022; Suzuki & Gottlieb, 2013). During distractor suppression, priority for specific distractors is reduced below a critical threshold (Serences, Yantis, Culberson & Awh, 2004). This implies that not all types of distractors are suppressed during search.

Several studies have explored the conditions in which a distractor can be suppressed which include color singleton distractors, luminance singleton distractor, predictable distractor (probabilistic learning) and task irrelevant distractors (Failing & Theeuwes, 2020; Wang, van Driel, Ort & Theeuwes, 2019). Some researchers claim that the effect of suppression is more pronounced in feature search than in singleton search (Bacon & Egeth, 1994; Chang & Egeth, 2021), because feature search allows subjects to use a strategy that can exclude salient objects from the attentional set whereas singleton search does not. This view has since then been challenged and the evidence seems inconclusive (Connor, Egeth & Yantis, 2004; Theeuwes, 2004). An increase in set size also influences the degree of suppression on a salient distractor such that smaller set sizes (<=4) facilitate suppression but larger set sizes (>=6) do not (Kerzel & Burra, 2020). Other factors like, statistical learning of distractor appearance, induced implicitly or explicitly as well as cue-based biasing also influences the degree of suppression (Britton & Anderson, 2020; Di Caro & Della Libera, 2021; Heuer & Schubö, 2020). So far it can be said that one can learn to suppress distractors with experience (reactively) but it is difficult to do so preemptively (proactively) without much experience with it. Studies are still exploring the role of working memory and control in suppression to clarify the processes through which suppression can manifest during selection. It is discussed in later sections of this chapter.

The term "suppression" has been used frequently in neurophysiological studies to indicate limiting a saccadic response (saccadic suppression) or a manual response (response suppression) to a target in the presence of a distractor (Eriksen & Hoffman, 1974; Greenwald, 1972). Since preparation of target-related response is delayed due to the preparation of distractor-related response, also called the psychological refractory period (Klapp, Maslovat & Jagacinski, 2019). However, this definition differs from the current definition of suppression which is a process that not only influences a late motoric response (decision making stages) but also the early attentive and preattentive stage of visual processing (Hamblin-Frohman, Chang, Egeth & Becker, 2022). Duncan and Humphreys (1992) first used the term suppression to suggest weighing down a group of distractors that differ significantly from the target template. On a *search surface* (now called attentional template), these weights are computed based on similarity between each search element and target template. When an item does not match the attentional template, it is marked as a distractor. If an element is similar to other search elements which are not the target, it again gets marked as a distractor. This allows suppression of a group of distractors at the same time, termed as *spreading suppression*. For instance, a salient distractor cannot be grouped with other distractors during search as it differs in one or more unique features and hence it receives less suppression than other distractions. Attention capture by such distractors observed during singleton search (Theeuwes, 1992) can also be explained by lack of suppression of the salient distractor.

2 Models of distractor inhibition

2.1 Historical overview

The focus of the current chapter is on distractor inhibition in visual search studies. However, questions regarding how and to what extent distractors can be avoided have long been of interest to researchers. Before we get into the current issues regarding distractor suppression, we will give a brief overview of the historical antecedents. Desimone and Duncan (1995) proposed the biased competition theory after having studied the ventral and dorsal neural pathways for selective attention. Filtering occurs as the neurons become more and more specialized along the pathway. Task goals, learning, reward, etc. play a role in biasing filtering by activating a combination of neurons. Targets fulfil the majority of criteria and win the competition whereas distractors do not and hence are filtered out. Salient distractors however capture attention, as shown in singleton search tasks (Theeuwes, 1992), implying that filtering is biased towards stimulus salience despite current goals. But the model suggests that stimuli are not only matched against target representations but also against currently perceived stimulus's representations, and hence biasing attention towards the target and away from distractors happens simultaneously.

Before this, Treisman and Sato (1990) had proposed the feature inhibition hypothesis assuming that task-irrelevant features can be ignored by suppressing one or more feature maps that the distractors are a part of. Similar-looking distractors can be suppressed parallelly. This was seen in a recent study by Won & Geng (2018) where they asked participants to perform a search task in two phases, training and testing. During the training phase, they observed distractors in fixed colors. In the testing phase, distractors appeared in two sets of colors, one closer to the trained colors (on a color wheel) and another far away. Faster RTs were observed when distractors of similar colors appeared compared to dissimilar colors. Thus, suppressing a color distractor facilitated the suppression of distractors of similar color. This idea has been utilized by Won et al. (2022) to propose a suppression template (similar to an attentional template) which comprises learned distractor features so that stimuli can be matched against it and suppressed faster instead of indulging in active consideration of all stimuli (Won & Geng, 2018).

The idea of suppression spreading from one distractor to another was explored further by Houghton and Tipper (1996). They found that the activated state of one system of neurons activates other systems connected to it unless prevented by inhibition from another neuron. Hence, inhibition is inevitable in selective attention. Building on the findings from Desimone and Duncan, they proposed a similar model suggesting that target selection is synchronous with the deselection of distractors (Tipper, Weaver & Houghton, 1994), with the exception of a feedback loop from working memory representations to perceptual representations. The role of the feedback loop was to allow the deselection of distractors by altering perceptual representations of items as they fail to match against target representations. Thus, suggesting that dynamic updating of attentional priority influences active perception. This may also suggest that perceptual awareness of objects progressively decreases as they get recognized as distractors. A recent study by Won, Venkatesh, Witkowski, Banh and Geng (2022) provided data which implied that memory representation of salient distractors diminished as learning of suppression progressed, further supporting that suppression is a perceptually dependent process.

Another form of suppression, called *expectation suppression*, is more selective to repeated occurrences of a specific distractor and can be explained by principles of predictive coding (see Noonan, Crittenden, Jensen & Stokes, 2018 for a detailed review comparing other forms of suppression). Predictive coding suggests that if task conditions remain relatively constant, and no novel information is added every trial, a baseline inhibition operates over all items. As a result, representations of the inhibited items no longer need to be maintained in the working memory. This form of suppression is also called repetition suppression since it is learned over repeated experiences with distractors. Predictive coding is similar to biased competition in the sense that perceptual representations are updated over time to diminish distractor representations but it differs in stating that this updating happens as a result of direct experience without involving the working memory. Lin et al. (2021) tested this idea by presenting a salient distractor more often in one location than another and found greater suppression at the high-probability distractor location compared to the low-probability distractor location (Lin, Li, Wang & Theeuwes, 2021). Another study by Noonan et al. (2016) measured ERPs while a target, a distractor or a neutral location was cued during a modified Posner's paradigm wherein the target was presented in one of the four quadrants while the distractor was presented in either blocked (50% trials) or randomized locations in the remaining three quadrants. Faster RTs on distractor cue vs neutral cue trials were observed only in the blocked condition but not in the randomized condition, suggesting that suppression relied on repetition learning and not on top-down control (Noonan, Adamian, Pike, Printzlau, Crittenden & Stokes, 2016).

2.2 *Current models*

Earlier accounts of suppression allowed a generalized suppression of a group of distractors. However, the *signal suppression hypothesis of controlled attention capture* proposed that salient distractors can be suppressed more than other distractors during feature search (Gaspelin, Leonard and Luck, 2015). In the feature search paradigm (see Figure 5.1 for a representative figure), participants are asked to find a target defined by a specific shape (circle/diamond) among different shape distractors (hexagon/square), all presented in, for example, green color. In half of the trials, one of the non-target shapes is presented in a unique color (red)

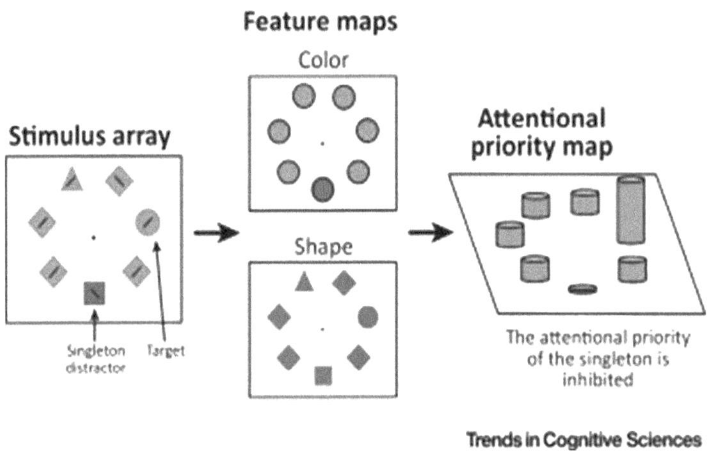

Figure 5.1 A sample feature search task and corresponding featural maps. Attentional priority map comprising of the combination of the two feature maps indicates low priority for the red singleton distractor and more high priority for the target shape.

which acts as a singleton distractor since it is unique in color (hence a singleton). The signal suppression hypothesis suggested that distractors that stand out in a certain feature (for instance unique color) compared to other distractors, generate an attend-to-me signal automatically (Theeuwes, 1992), which allows bottom-up capture of attention by the singleton. Such capture can be prevented by top-down control if the singleton does not match the target template in any feature or when the singleton detection mode is discouraged during search. Singleton detection mode is encouraged when the target is a unique shape, such as a diamond among all circles (or vice versa). Hence, participants tend to search for any singleton (red shape among green shapes or diamond among circles) instead of searching for a predefined feature (like circle or diamond). During feature search, however, all shapes are different and hence search strategy is specific to the target shape and the singleton-detection mode is discouraged. As a result, the attend-to-me signal of the singleton distractor can be suppressed.

Gaspelin, Leonard and Luck (2015) demonstrated signal suppression using a modified feature search task. Response times for finding the target were compared across two types of trials, singleton distractor present trials and singleton distractor absent trials. In the former, a unique color singleton distractor appears during search whereas all distractors match the target color in later trials. If the singleton distractor is suppressed during feature search, RTs must be faster on singleton present trials than on singleton absent trials, which was demonstrated in the study. Additionally, probe trials were intermixed with search trials. On probe trials, alphabets were superimposed on search shapes for 100 ms and participants were asked to recall as many alphabets as they could post the display disappeared. In these trials, search for the target shape was not required, hence any biases towards the target or the against salient distractor were expected to affect the recall accuracy of probe letters on the corresponding shapes. They found that probe recall accuracy depended on the objects being probed (target, singleton distractor or non-singleton distractor), such that. probes at the singleton distractor location were recalled with 6% (and 12% and 8% in experiments 3 and 4, respectively) less accuracy than probes at the average non-singleton distractor, in experiment 2, thus supporting signal suppression at the singleton distractor location (Gaspelin, Leonard & Luck, 2015) compared to non-singleton distractor locations.

The signal suppression hypothesis proposes the possibility of suppression of a singleton distractor however, it does not explain what gets suppressed and why. Below we will discuss potential models of suppression, distinguished based on the criteria of what is suppressed. The *first-order suppression* model suggests that attention is guided by specific features of objects and hence suppression of an object must entail the suppression of the specific feature (e.e., red, blue). This entails that first-order suppression operates on first-order featural maps (Gaspelin & Luck, 2018) for color, orientation, luminance, motion, etc., presumably at a preattentive level (Treisman & Gelade, 1980). Gaspelin and Luck (2018) tested the assumptions of first-order suppression by hypothesizing that knowing specific features of singleton distractor is necessary to suppress it. In Experiment 1, the task was similar to the task in Gaspelin et al. (2015) with the exception that the singleton and non-singleton colors were swapped unpredictably across trials. If the color of the singleton cannot be guessed before the trial, suppression must not be possible in this experiment, which was demonstrated by slower RTs on singleton present trials than singleton absent trials. In experiments 2 and 3 the color swapping happened in blocks and similar results were observed. In experiment 4, only the color of the singleton distractor was swapped keeping the color of the non-singleton distractors constant. Suppression of the singleton distractor was observed in the fourth quarter block, after sufficiently learning the color of the singleton distractor, providing support for first-order suppression.

The feature of an upcoming singleton cannot be predicted all the time. Does this mean that an unpredictable distractor cannot be suppressed as suggested by first-order suppression? An alternative account, *second-order suppression* suggests that feature discontinuities among first-order feature maps are also used to guide attention and hence suppression of a distractor necessitates the detection of feature discontinuities (Gaspelin & Luck, 2018) and not the specific feature. For instance, a red distractor among green non-targets can be suppressed by discarding any color singleton, without suppressing the specific color (red). In a modified search task, Ma and Abrams (2022), showed that an unpredictable color singleton can be suppressed during feature search if the task strategy does not prioritize singular elements in the display, like a singleton. Much like Bacon and Egeth (1994), they encouraged participants to look for a shape that was more in number in a search display (circles or squares), thus promoting the search for a group of items instead of singular items. This change in strategy resulted in the suppression of singular items like the color singleton, despite participants not being able to predict its color on a given trial. The RTs were faster in the presence of the singleton distractor than in its absence, and probe recall accuracy was significantly low at the singleton distractor location, supporting second-order suppression.

Another potential mechanism of suppression similar to second-order suppression is the dimensional weighing account. It predicts that visual attention can be configured to value one featureal dimension more over another which is comparable to suppressing distractor with featural discontinuities as suggested in second-order suppression. However, here the suppression operates at a dimensional level not at the level of second-order featural maps. For example, when a participant searches for a circle among among diamonds and an irrelevant color singleton appears in an unpredictable color, it is possible to ignore featural discontinuities in the color dimension and enhance those in shape dimension. Hence, if the color dimension can be weighed down relative to the shape dimension (Found & Müller, 1996; Müller, Heller & Ziegler, 1995; Müller, Reimann & Krummenacher, 2003). Not many studies have supported the dimensional weighing account since its conception, hence it cannot be proposed as a notable hypothesis. However, it supports the possibility of a (second-order) suppression-like process. The experimental evidence discussed above highlights two important aspects of suppression. First, it highlights the importance of featural maps in suppression. Second, it suggests that suppression is guided by a range of strategies depending upon the task demands.

Taken together, these accounts suggest a target template (or attentional template) which encodes target representations from foreknowledge or active visual processing. All models reach convergence in suggesting that distractor representations are updated during search but disagree on its dependance on working memory to facilitate suppression (Gao & Theeuwes, 2020). Alongside these, findings from Donnelly, Humphreys and Riddoch (1991), suggested that preattentive features combine into a primitive object description which guides search. And Treisman (1992) suggested that different feature maps have separate effects at the preattentive level. This opens up a new line of investigation into the role of consciousness in attentional processing of distractors (Chisholm & Kingstone, 2014; Prasad & Mishra, 2019). If working memory representations are not needed for suppression, where are distractors represented and maintained during search? How is suppression generalized across similar distractors? Many studies have induced suppression implicitly by creating a probabilistic expectation of distractor appearance over the course of several trials (Leber, Gwinn, Hong & O'Toole, 2016; Theeuwes, Bogaerts & van Moorselaar, 2022). A few studies have also tried to use subliminal cues to enhance suppression of feature matching distractors. Using both approaches, the participants remain unaware that the distractor is being suppressed and yet they suppress it consistently (Gao & Theeuwes, 2022). In fact, increasing awareness about the distractor makes it difficult to suppress (Adams & Gaspelin, 2020). Some of these critical findings are discussed in detail in the next section with respect to the explicit role of unconscious processes during suppression.

3 Theoretical support for unconscious distractor inhibition

Desimone and Duncan (1995) suggested that subjects are aware of the contents of attended stimuli and unaware of the contents of unattended stimuli. In their model, distractors lose the competition and hence remain unattended. This implies that subjects may be unaware of distractors while they are looking for the target. While it does not seem plausible to think that rejection of an object can happen without consciously perceiving it. The biased competition theory predicts that unattended stimuli (distractors) do not demand processing capacity. It is hence safe to assume that the model suggests an unconscious process of distractor filtering while target enhancement must proceed with conscious awareness. The idea of "spreading suppression," first explored by Duncan and Humphreys (1992) and later by Houghton and Tipper (1996), would then imply that distractor representations are actively perceived and suppressed parallelly for similar distractors and serially for singleton distractors. But such a process will need a storage facility to match representations. Coltheart (1983) proposed that iconic memory is used for the early visual processes also assumed to be automatic and unconscious. It was characteristic of a large capacity and extremely short decay time. Hence, tasks that measure memory traces of such process often indicated no evidence for it. Allport (1989) also suggested that iconic memory can contain visual features such as color, orientation or even letters, numerals and familiar words. Crick and Koch (1990) proposed that iconic memory involves rapid synaptic modifications which are maintained on their own, like a default neuronal process. Taken together, the biased competition model and older ideas on preattentive cognition suggest that distractor processing relies on updating of iconic memory representations and can take place for an array of distractors parallelly but is short lived.

Houghton and Tipper (1996) proposed that working memory is utilized to store a suppression template which updates perceptual input based of features identified as distractors, also aligning with concept of expectation suppression proposed by predictive coding. While they have no direct motivation for assuming the role of working memory in this process, recent evidence of learned suppression of distractors supports this claim. Several studies have shown that observing distractor at a location consistently helps in avoiding it the next time it appears there. Such learning is takes place quickly and stays as long as the experience with distractor does not change. Other studies discussed earlier also showed that learning of one distractor appearance contingency can be overridden by another in due course of time. Such dynamic shifting of biases will most likely require resources from the working memory. Thus, we can say that distractor suppression is not a unitary process, rather a combination of processes that may or may not consume working memory. If the task demands a dynamic shift in suppression strategy, working memory based suppression must be preferred but if suppression of a large number of similar distractors is needed a parallel process running in iconic memory must be sufficient to guide search. Current conceptualization of suppression into types such as first-order and second-order, also relies on the role of working memory in suppression (Gaspelin & Luck, 2018). For instance, first-order suppression entails suppression of specific task irrelevant feature. Whereas second-order suppression allows suppression of any feature that may be task irrelevant. In that sense, first order suppression is object oriented while second-order suppression is generalized across visual field. Taken together we suggest that task demands decide if the suppression of distractors must be perform using first-order processes, utilizing working memory (Beck & Hollingworth, 2015) or using second-order processes without the need for updating memory representations (Beck, Luck & Hollingworth, 2018).

4 Experimental evidence for unconscious distractor inhibition

4.1 Evidence from statistical learning studies

A majority of the evidence for unconscious inhibition of distractor locations comes from statistical learning studies. Learning from experience that a certain feature is associated with a task-irrelevant distractor, guides suppression (Britton & Anderson, 2020; Gottlieb, 2012; Jiang & Sisk, 2019). Probabilistic cueing of irrelevant distractor locations over a period of time can generate implicit bias (Leber, Gwinn, Hong & O'Toole, 2016). For instance, Di Caro, Theeuwes and Della Libera (2019) asked observers to view an array of six gray-colored circles in an additional singleton search. After 500–800 ms all circles turned green except one, indicating that it was the target. Observers were asked to discriminate the orientation of a line on the target. On some trials an additional color singleton appeared between any two search items. In one block, the probability of the additional singleton appearing in two locations was higher than the remaining four locations (biased phase) and was equally likely at all locations in another block (unbiased phase). Reduced capture was seen when the additional singleton appeared at high probability locations compared to the low probability locations but only in the biased phase. No difference was observed between different singleton locations in the unbiased phase. Only four out of 24 participants reported high probability distractor locations correctly, at the end of the task. Whereas others were aware of a bias but could not detect the high probability location with confidence. This suggests that although distractor suppression varied as a function of the learned distractor probability, it was independent of awareness of the learning. Several other studies have found similar results (Ferrante, Patacca, Di Caro, Santandrea, Della Libera & Chelazzi, 2017; Wang & Theeuwes, 2018).

In a version of the singleton search task, Wang and Theeuwes (2018) asked participants to report the orientation of a line on a diamond (or circle, counterbalanced across participants) target while a singleton color distractor appeared on 66% trials at a high probability location (on 65% trials) or at any of the low probability locations (on 35% trials). Search RTs varied across locations as a function of salient distractor probability such that a gradient of

RTs was observed. Fastest RTs were observed when a distractor appeared at the high probability distractor location and slowest when it appeared at the low probability location. However, when asked to report the high probability location, participants failed to do so suggesting that the learning happened implicitly or without conscious awareness. In another study, Wang and Theeuwes (2020) modified the task to investigate if the learned bias can also be altered during a task. After a block of trials the high probability location shifted to another position of the search display and continued for the respective block. This was followed by a third shift in high probability distractor location. The response time plotted as a function of blocks indicated over all faster RTs when the distractor appeared at the high probability location of each block compared to the low probability location. Moreover, faster RTs were observed for high probability locations in the respective block and not for the location which had highest probability in the previous block (Wang & Theeuwes, 2020). Despite the dynamic adjustment in distractor location probability, participants did not gain awareness of this change and overall failed to report the high probability location accurately. These studies together suggest that suppression of distractor locations is implicit and can be dynamically adjusted.

While the above-mentioned studies provide evidence for the implicit nature of spatial distractor suppression, similar evidence for feature-based suppression based on implicit statistical regularities is not as clear. To examine if statistical regularities in features can modulate distractor suppression, Stilwell, Bahle and Vecera (2019) administered a search task where participants were asked to find a green circle (target) in a display containing green diamonds and sometimes, a salient distractor. Crucially, the salient distractor was more likely to be presented in one color (example: red) than in another (example: yellow). The objective was to examine if regularities in the distractor feature influence suppression the same way regularities in locations have been shown to influence.

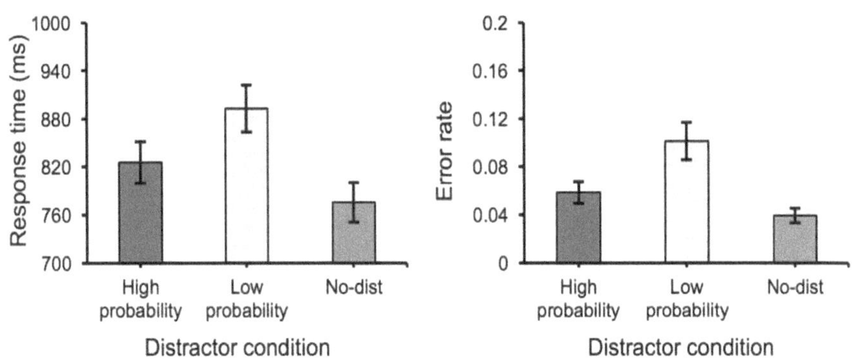

Figure 5.2 Average RT and error rates for experiment 1 in Wang and Theeuwes (2018), showed faster RTs for salient distractor appearing at high probability location than low probability location. Error rates, replicated a similar pattern of results.

The results found this to be true. High-probability distractors could be avoided more easily than the low-probability distractors. However, it is worth noting that this study did not assess awareness of the regularities of the distractor color so it is not clear if this indeed demonstrates unconscious suppression.

4.2 Evidence from unconscious cueing studies

Subliminal cues can influence inhibitory processes (Eimer & Schlaghecken, 2003). In a recent study by Gamble and Song (2016), participants searched for a singleton target in the presence of a fixed number of consciously and unconsciously perceived distractors. Increasing the number of unconscious distractors slowed down reaction times to the target significantly. Thus, the selection of the target necessitated filtering of not only consciously perceived distractors but also unconsciously perceived distractors. This suggests that visual search involves simultaneous conscious and unconscious processing that influences the selection of the target. Ansorge et al. (2009) also found that targets cued by a conscious valid cue and an unconscious valid cue, both enhance RTs (Ansorge, Kiss & Eimer, 2009). However, in another study Ansorge, Horstmann and Worschech (2010) found that masked cues captured attention when they matched task-relevant features (target color), but not when they matched task-irrelevant features (distractor colors). Thus, subliminal cues influence selection processes in the same way as conscious cues (i.e., task-relevant cues benefit selection and task-irrelevant cues do not). This raises the possibility that attentional control operating on conscious perception is similar to attentional control operating on unconscious perception. But we also know that task-irrelevant distractors can be suppressed when attentional control settings do not favor capture by singleton distractors. Hence, cueing the location of a suppressed distractor can help in its suppression. While this has not been demonstrated in many search studies, priming the distractor or negative priming has been shown to enhance performance (Tipper, 1985). This may suggest that unconscious processes of inhibition are more influential on late-motoric/response processes compared to early-attentional processes.

Further examination of unconscious task-irrelevant cues was seen in a study by Lamy, Alon, Carmel and Shalev (2015), using a modified spatial cueing paradigm. They subjected participants to a color target search while a color singleton cue preceded it. The awareness of the cue was manipulated in experiments 1 and 2 using continuous flash suppression and in experiment 3 using brief presentation (40 ms). The cue location matched the target location on 50% of trials and appeared at a different location on the remaining trials. When Response times were compared between valid and invalid cues for the target color cues, standard cueing effects were observed (faster RT on valid trials). However, when the cue color was different than the target color, a same-location cost was observed (slower RT on valid trials). This was seen only for conscious cues, whereas unconscious cues did not incur the same-location cost for the color-mismatching cues. Lamy et al. (2015) suggested that the cost is a result of a cascade of processes such as updating the memory representation of the perceived cue, matching it with the target representation and deciding that it is a mismatch. They suggested that this may not occur for unconscious cues since conscious awareness is critical for forming memory representations, and conversely unconsciously perceived cues do not create representations in memory. Hence, there was no need to update cue representations when the unconscious cue color did not match the target color.

Further investigation into this was done by Travis, Dux and Mattingley (2019) by using the same design as Lamy et al. (2015) and additionally measuring ERPs. The manual responses partly replicated Lamy et al. (2015) such that the same location benefit was independent of conscious awareness of the cues. However, the same location cost for irrelevant color cues was seen for both aware and unaware cues. This finding was further replicated in ERPs which did not show any difference in PD elicited by aware and unaware distractor cues suggesting that suppression of visual features does not require conscious awareness. It remains to be explored if the degree of suppression differs with and without awareness of the to-be-suppressed stimuli. If unconsciously perceived cues allowed greater goal-directed control it could explain why irrelevant cues produced less cost in the unaware condition of Lamy et al. (2015). It is difficult to reconcile the discrepancies between Lamy et al. (2015) and Travis et al. (2019) since the findings have not been replicated any further but we can imply that attentional processing with and without awareness is controlled by dynamic and complex attentional control processes. More investigations into this issue must look at different types of unconscious cues, featural or spatial, endogenous or exogenous, central or peripheral such that the findings can explain the process operating in tandem to influence attentional selection.

In an ongoing study, Mohite and Mishra aimed to investigate if brief cues (presented for 16 ms), perceived subliminally can enhance the suppression of a salient distractor (data not yet published). In one such study, a centrally presented subliminal cue appeared before a feature search task, where the color of the cue matched either the target color, the salient distractor color or a neutral color in a given block of trials. Participants were asked to report the orientation of a line of the target shape (circle/diamond) while ignoring the singleton distractor that appeared only in 50% of the total trials (always in the same color). The difference in response time to target on distractor present and absent trials indicated suppression and was observed in all cue blocks except the distractor color cue block. This suggested that a distractor matching cue before search hampers suppression of the distractor during search. While this finding can indicate that distractor-matching subliminal cues do not enhance suppression, findings from this particular study could also be explained by the difficulty in disengaging from the central cue, especially when it matched the distractor. In another study, Mohite and Mishra explored this using additional eye-tracking measures. The distractor color-matching cues were presented at all search locations instead of the center such that the cue only influences the feature map of the upcoming singleton distractor. Additionally, a distractor location matching cue was presented at the upcoming salient distractor location (in a neutral color) and a distractor color matching cue was presented at the upcoming salient distractor location. These two conditions influenced the attentional processing of the distractor at the spatial and both featural and spatial levels, respectively. Response times suggested the maximum benefit of color cues for suppression while the proportion of eye movements showed greater oculomotor suppression for location and both (color and location) matching cues.

Overall, the studies discussed above suggest that unconscious biases induced by probabilistic learning or explicit cueing last until learning is consistent and the cue is useful. This suggests that implicit learning is very precise although unconscious. The attentional biases created as a result of this learning are stable until the conditions causing the biases remain constant. Any change in the probabilistic expectations affects learning without letting the agent gain conscious awareness of the change in expectations. Implicit learning can also dynamically adjust to benefit suppression, provided sufficient time is provided for the newly learned contingencies to set in. Similar control over attentional guidance is observed in paradigms that use subliminal cues that match distractor or task-irrelevant features. These cues tend to reduce or nullify the cost of invalid cueing and offer the same benefit of valid cueing as consciously perceived cues. When Mohite and Mishra compared distractor cueing between subliminal and visible cues, the benefits offered by color-matching cues were similar, suggesting that the cue enhanced suppression of the salient distractor irrespective of its awareness. EEG and eye-tracking data provided by Travis et al. (2019) and Mohite and Mishra offer some preliminary insights into the complex interaction between awareness and attention. Travis et al. (2019) found that target enhancement was better with aware cues than unaware cues, but distractor suppression remained unaffected. This could suggest that inhibitory mechanisms of selection are getting influenced by unconscious processes as much as by conscious processes while the same is not true for excitatory processes of selection. Further, Mohite and Mishra suggest that comparing suppression of oculomotor responses and manual responses for aware and unaware cues might shed light on the dissociation in the attentional control processes and motor responses that needs to be further examined.

5 Concluding remarks and future research questions

We have reviewed existing evidence in favor of unconscious distractor suppression. There is overwhelming evidence from statistical learning studies that distractor suppression may proceed even in the absence of conscious awareness. Lack of awareness is typically established by asking participants if they noticed any regularities to which they respond with a yes/no answer. However, there have been questions on whether participants are truly unaware of the probability manipulations in such studies (Giménez-Fernández, Luque, Shanks & Vadillo, 2020; Vicente-Conesa, Giménez-Fernández, Luque & Vadillo, 2023). For instance, Vicente-Conesa et al. (2023) used a rating scale (with 6 options) rather than eliciting a binary response. They showed that many participants responded "possibly yes" when asked if the salient distractor had appeared more frequently in one particular location suggesting that claims of lack of awareness could depend on the method used to measure it. Having a reliable method for establishing the lack of conscious awareness has been notoriously difficult and is one of the enduring problems in research on unconscious processing (Francken et al., 2022; Sandberg, Timmermans, Overgaard & Cleeremans, 2010). It is necessary for future studies to follow the debates in the unconscious perception literature and use sensitive measures of awareness in probability learning studies.

One of the critical questions with no clear answers is how a suppression strategy gets selected for a certain search task. Attentional control processes regulate the availability of attention and working memory resources for a given task and hence help in choosing a strategy for search. In the case of distractor suppression, the availability of working memory resources decides the suppression strategy. Since, attentional control is subjected to individual differences arising as a result of factors like age, gender, psychopathology and culture; it is natural to expect that suppression varies as a result of these factors as well. Future studies can explore the various factors using modified versions of the visual search paradigm. Additionally, to understand the neurocognitive processes involved in suppression, it is necessary to study the brain basis of this process as it may arise actively during a task. So far studies have measured ERPs and fMRI scans during suppression to measure distractor positivity or Pd and localize brain regions for suppression. However, the lack of sufficient data does not allow much credibility to current neurological correlates of distractor suppression. To address this, along with a replication of existing studies, neuroimaging in animal models displaying processes similar to suppression will help trace the evolutionary origin and need for suppression.

References

Adams, O. J. & Gaspelin, N. (2020). Assessing introspective awareness of attention capture. *Attention, Perception & Psychophysics*, 82(4), 1586–1598.

Adams, O. J. & Gaspelin, N. (2021). Introspective awareness of oculomotor attentional capture. *Journal of Experimental Psychology: Human Perception and Performance*, 47 (3), 442.

Allport, A. (1989). Visual attention. In M. I. Posner (Ed.), *Foundations of cognitive science* (pp. 631–682). MIT Press.

Ansorge, U., Kiss, M. & Eimer, M. (2009). Goal-driven attentional capture by invisible colors: Evidence from event-related potentials. *Psychonomic Bulletin & Review*, 16(4), 648–653. https://doi.org/10.3758/pbr.16.4.648.

Ansorge, U., Horstmann, G. & Worschech, F. (2010). Attentional capture by masked colour singletons. *Vision Research*, 50(19), 2015–2027.

Bacon, W. F. & Egeth, H. E. (1994). Overriding stimulus-driven attentional capture. *Perception & Psychophysics*, 55(5), 485–496.

Beck, V. M. & Hollingworth, A. (2015). Evidence for negative feature guidance in visual search is explained by spatial recoding. *Journal of Experimental Psychology: Human Perception and Performance*, 41(5), 1190.

Beck, V. M., Luck, S. J. & Hollingworth, A. (2018). Whatever you do, don't look at the...: Evaluating guidance by an exclusionary attentional template. *Journal of Experimental Psychology: Human Perception and Performance*, 44(4), 645.

Bichot, N. P., Rossi, A. F. & Desimone, R. (2005). Parallel and serial neural mechanisms for visual search in macaque area V4. *Science*, 308(5721), 529–534.

Britton, M. K. & Anderson, B. A. (2020). Specificity and persistence of statistical learning in distractor suppression. *Journal of Experimental Psychology: Human Perception and Performance*, 46(3), 324.

Broadbent, D. E. (1982). Task combination and selective intake of information. *Acta Psychologica*, 50(3), 253–290.

Broadbent, D. E. (2013). *Perception and communication*. Elsevier.

Burra, N. & Kerzel, D. (2014). The distractor positivity (Pd) signals lowering of attentional priority: Evidence from event-related potentials and individual differences. *Psychophysiology*, 51(7), 685–696.

Chang, S. & Egeth, H. E. (2021). Can salient stimuli really be suppressed?. *Attention, Perception & Psychophysics*, 83(1), 260–269.

Chisholm, J. D. & Kingstone, A. (2014). Knowing and avoiding: The influence of distractor awareness on oculomotor capture. *Attention, Perception & Psychophysics*, 76 (5), 1258–1264.

Christie, J. J. & Klein, R. M. (2008). On finding negative priming from distractors. *Psychonomic Bulletin & Review*, 15(4), 866–873.

Coltheart, M. (1983). Iconic memory. *Philosophical Transactions of the Royal Society of London. B, Biological Sciences*, 302(1110), 283–294.

Connor, C. E., Egeth, H. E. & Yantis, S. (2004). Visual attention: bottom-up versus top-down. *Current Biology*, 14(19), R850–R852.

Crick, F. & Koch, C. (1990). Towards a neurobiological theory of consciousness. In *Seminars in the neurosciences* (vol. 2, pp. 263–275). Saunders Scientific Publications.

Desimone, R. & Duncan, J. (1995). Neural mechanisms of selective visual attention. *Annual Review of Neuroscience*, 18(1), 193–222.

Di Caro, V. & Della Libera, C. (2021). Statistical learning of target selection and distractor suppression shape attentional priority according to different timeframes. *Scientific Reports*, 11(1), 1–14.

Di Caro, V., Theeuwes, J. & Della Libera, C. (2019). Suppression history of distractor location biases attentional and oculomotor control. *Visual Cognition*, 27(2), 142–157.

Donnelly, N., Humphreys, G. W. & Riddoch, M. J. (1991). Parallel computation of primitive shape descriptions. *Journal of Experimental Psychology: Human Perception and Performance*, 17(2), 561.

Duncan, J. & Humphreys, G. (1992). Beyond the search surface: visual search and attentional engagement. *Journal of Experimental Psychology: Human Perception and Performance*, 18, 578–588.

Eimer, M. & Schlaghecken, F. (2003). Response facilitation and inhibition in subliminal priming. *Biological Psychology*, 64(1–2), 7–26.

Eriksen, C. W. & Hoffman, J. E. (1974). Selective attention: Noise suppression or signal enhancement?. *Bulletin of the Psychonomic Society*, 4(6), 587–589.

Failing, M. & Theeuwes, J. (2020). More capture, more suppression: Distractor suppression due to statistical regularities is determined by the magnitude of attentional capture. *Psychonomic Bulletin & Review*, 27(1), 86–95.

Failing, M., Wang, B. & Theeuwes, J. (2019). Spatial suppression due to statistical regularities is driven by distractor suppression not by target activation. *Attention, Perception & Psychophysics*, 81(5), 1405–1414.

Feldmann-Wüstefeld, T., Weinberger, M. & Awh, E. (2021). Spatially guided distractor suppression during visual search. *Journal of Neuroscience*, 41(14), 3180–3191.

Ferrante, O., Patacca, A., Di Caro, V., Santandrea, E., Della Libera, C. & Chelazzi, L. (2017). Statistical learning of distractor suppression. *Journal of Vision*, 17(10), 674.

Findlay, J. M. (1997). Saccade target selection during visual search. *Vision Research*, 37 (5), 617–631.

Folk, C. L., Remington, R. W. & Wright, J. H. (1994). The structure of attentional control: contingent attentional capture by apparent motion, abrupt onset, and colour. *Journal of Experimental Psychology: Human Perception and Performance*, 20(2), 317.

Found, A. & Müller, H. J. (1996). Searching for unknown feature targets on more than one dimension: Investigating a "dimension-weighting" account. *Perception & Psychophysics*, 58(1), 88–101.

Francken, J., Beerendonk, L., Molenaar, D., Fahrenfort, J., Kiverstein, J., Seth, A. & van Gaal, S. (2022). An academic survey on theoretical foundations, common assumptions and the current state of consciousness science. *Neuroscience of Consciousness*, 2022 (1), niac011.

Gamble, C. & Song, J. H. (2016). Impact of conscious versus unconscious distractors in pop-out visual search. *Journal of Vision*, 16(12), 1319.

Gao, Y. & Theeuwes, J. (2020). Learning to suppress a distractor is not affected by working memory load. *Psychonomic Bulletin & Review*, 27(1), 96–104.

Gao, Y. & Theeuwes, J. (2022). Learning to suppress a location does not depend on knowing which location. *Attention, Perception & Psychophysics*, 84(4), 1087–1097.

Gaspelin, N., Leonard, C. J. & Luck, S. J. (2015). Direct evidence for active suppression of salient-but-irrelevant sensory inputs. *Psychological Science*, 26(11), 1740–1750.

Gaspelin, N. & Luck, S. J. (2018). Distinguishing among potential mechanisms of singleton suppression. *Journal of Experimental Psychology: Human Perception and Performance*, 44(4), 626.

Geng, J. J. (2014). Attentional mechanisms of distractor suppression. *Current Directions in Psychological Science*, 23(2), 147–153.

Giménez-Fernández, T., Luque, D., Shanks, D. R. & Vadillo, M. A. (2020). Probabilistic cuing of visual search: Neither implicit nor inflexible. *Journal of Experimental Psychology: Human Perception and Performance*, 46(10), 1222.

Gottlieb, J. (2012). Attention, learning, and the value of information. *Neuron*, 76(2), 281–295.

Greenwald, A. G. (1972). Evidence of both perceptual filtering and response suppression for rejected messages in selective attention. *Journal of Experimental Psychology*, 94(1), 58.

Hamblin-Frohman, Z., Chang, S., Egeth, H. & Becker, S. I. (2022). Eye movements reveal the contributions of early and late processes of enhancement and suppression to the guidance of visual search. *Attention, Perception & Psychophysics*, 84(6), 1913–1924.

Heuer, A. & Schubö, A. (2020). Cueing distraction: electrophysiological evidence for anticipatory active suppression of distractor location. *Psychological Research*, 84(8), 2111–2121.

Hickey, C., Di Lollo, V. & McDonald, J. J. (2009). Electrophysiological indices of target and distractor processing in visual search. *Journal of Cognitive Neuroscience*, 21(4), 760–775.

Houghton, G. & Tipper, S. P. (1996). Inhibitory mechanisms of neural and cognitive control: Applications to selective attention and sequential action. *Brain and Cognition*, 30(1), 20–43.

Itti, L. & Koch, C. (2001). Computational modelling of visual attention. *Nature Reviews Neuroscience*, 2(3), 194–203.

Jiang, Y. V. & Sisk, C. A. (2019). Habit-like attention. *Current Opinion in Psychology*, 29, 65–70.

Kerzel, D. & Burra, N. (2020). Capture by context elements, not attentional suppression of distractors, explains the PD with small search displays. *Journal of Cognitive Neuroscience*, 32(6), 1170–1183.

Klapp, S. T., Maslovat, D. & Jagacinski, R. J. (2019). The bottleneck of the psychological refractory period effect involves timing of response initiation rather than response selection. *Psychonomic Bulletin & Review*, 26(1), 29–47.

Lamy, D., Alon, L., Carmel, T., & Shalev, N. (2015). The role of conscious perception in attentional capture and object-file updating. *Psychological Science*, 26(1), 48–57.

Leber, A. B., Gwinn, R. E., Hong, Y. & O'Toole, R. J. (2016). Implicitly learned suppression of irrelevant spatial locations. *Psychonomic Bulletin & Review*, 23, 1873–1881.

Liesefeld, H. R., Liesefeld, A. M., Töllner, T. & Müller, H. J. (2017). Attentional capture in visual search: Capture and post-capture dynamics revealed by EEG. *NeuroImage*, 156, 166–173.

Lin, R., Li, X., Wang, B. & Theeuwes, J. (2021). Spatial suppression due to statistical learning tracks the estimated spatial probability. *Attention, Perception & Psychophysics*, 83(1), 283–291.

Ma, X. & Abrams, R. A. (2022). Ignoring the unknown: Attentional suppression of unpredictable visual distraction. *Journal of Experimental Psychology: Human Perception and Performance.*

Müller, H. J., Heller, D. & Ziegler, J. (1995). Visual search for singleton feature targets within and across feature dimensions. *Perception & Psychophysics*, 57(1), 1–17.

Müller, H. J., Reimann, B. & Krummenacher, J. (2003). Visual search for singleton feature targets across dimensions: Stimulus- and expectancy-driven effects in dimensional weighting. *Journal of Experimental Psychology: Human Perception and Performance*, 29(5), 1021–1035.

Noonan, M. P., Adamian, N., Pike, A., Printzlau, F., Crittenden, B. M. & Stokes, M. G. (2016). Distinct mechanisms for distractor suppression and target facilitation. *Journal of Neuroscience*, 36(6), 1797–1807.

Noonan, M. P., Crittenden, B. M., Jensen, O. & Stokes, M. G. (2018). Selective inhibition of distracting input. *Behavioural Brain Research*, 355, 36–47.

Prasad, S. & Mishra, R. K. (2019). The nature of unconscious attention to subliminal cues. *Vision*, 3(3), 38.

Sandberg, K., Timmermans, B., Overgaard, M. & Cleeremans, A. (2010). Measuring consciousness: is one measure better than the other? *Consciousness and Cognition*, 19 (4), 1069–1078.

Sawaki, R. & Luck, S. J. (2010). Capture versus suppression of attention by salient singletons: Electrophysiological evidence for an automatic attend-to-me signal. *Attention, Perception & Psychophysics*, 72(6), 1455–1470.

Schneider, D., Herbst, S. K., Klatt, L. I. & Wöstmann, M. (2022). Target enhancement or distractor suppression? Functionally distinct alpha oscillations form the basis of attention. *European Journal of Neuroscience*, 55(11–12), 3256–3265.

Serences, J. T., Yantis, S., Culberson, A. & Awh, E. (2004). Preparatory activity in visual cortex indexes distractor suppression during covert spatial orienting. *Journal of Neurophysiology*, 92(6), 3538–3545.

Stilwell, B. T., Bahle, B. & Vecera, S. P. (2019). Feature-based statistical regularities of distractors modulate attentional capture. *Journal of Experimental Psychology: Human Perception and Performance*, 45(3), 419.

Suzuki, M. & Gottlieb, J. (2013). Distinct neural mechanisms of distractor suppression in the frontal and parietal lobe. *Nature Neuroscience*, 16(1), 98–104.

Theeuwes, J. (1992). Perceptual selectivity for color and form. *Perception & Psychophysics*, 51(6), 599–606.

Theeuwes, J. (2004). Top-down search strategies cannot override attentional capture. *Psychonomic Bulletin & Review*, 11(1), 65–70.

Theeuwes, J., Bogaerts, L. & van Moorselaar, D. (2022). What to expect where and when: How statistical learning drives visual selection. Trends in Cognitive Sciences, 26(10), 860–872.

Tipper, S. P. (1985). The negative priming effect: Inhibitory priming by ignored objects. *The Quarterly Journal of Experimental Psychology*, 37(4), 571–590.

Tipper, S. P. (2001). Does negative priming reflect inhibitory mechanisms? A review and integration of conflicting views. *The Quarterly Journal of Experimental Psychology Section A*, 54(2), 321–343.

Tipper, S. P., Weaver, B. & Houghton, G. (1994). Behavioural goals determine inhibitory mechanisms of selective attention. *The Quarterly Journal of Experimental Psychology Section A*, 47(4), 809–840.

Travis, S. L., Dux, P. E. & Mattingley, J. B. (2019). Neural correlates of goal-directed enhancement and suppression of visual stimuli in the absence of conscious perception. *Attention, Perception & Psychophysics*, 81, 1346–1364.

Treisman, A. & Gelade, G. (1980). A feature-integration theory of attention. *Cognitive Psychology*, 12(1), 97–136.

Treisman, A. & Sato, S. (1990). Conjunction search revisited. *Journal of Experimental Psychology: Human Perception and Performance*, 16(3), 459.

Vicente-Conesa, F., Giménez-Fernández, T., Luque, D. & Vadillo, M. A. (2023). Learning to suppress a distractor may not be unconscious. *Attention, Perception & Psychophysics*, 85, 796–813.

Wang, B. & Theeuwes, J. (2018). Statistical regularities modulate attentional capture. *Journal of Experimental Psychology: Human Perception and Performance*, 44(1), 13.

Wang, B. & Theeuwes, J. (2020). Implicit attentional biases in a changing environment. *Acta Psychologica*, 206, 103064.

Wang, B., van Driel, J., Ort, E. & Theeuwes, J. (2019). Anticipatory distractor suppression elicited by statistical regularities in visual search. *Journal of Cognitive Neuroscience*, 31(10), 1535–1548.

Won, B. Y. & Geng, J. J. (2018). Learned suppression for multiple distractors in visual search. *Journal of Experimental Psychology: Human Perception and Performance*, 44(7), 1128.

Won, B. Y., Venkatesh, A., Witkowski, P. P., Banh, T. & Geng, J. J. (2022). Memory precision for salient distractors decreases with learned suppression. *Psychonomic Bulletin & Review*, 29(1), 169–181.

Zhang, X. (1999). *Anticipatory inhibition: An intentional nonspatial mechanism revealed with the distractor previewing technique*. Princeton University Press.

Ziaei, M. & Fischer, H. (2016). Emotion and ageing: the impact of emotion on attention, memory, and face recognition in late adulthood. In J. R. Absher & J. Cloutier (Eds.), *Neuroimaging personality, social cognition, and character* (pp. 259–278). Academic Press.

6 The functional role of the oculomotor system in spatial short-term memory

Siobhan McAteer, Soazig Casteau and Daniel T. Smith

1. History

Interest in the functional role of eye movements in visuospatial short-term memory arose from a desire to address two key questions about the nature of visuospatial short-term memory (henceforth VSSTM). Firstly, given that perception arises from integrating perceptual information across sequences of fixations, how does the system encode and store the spatial properties of the visual information arising from each fixation in a way that preserves their relative spatial relationships. Secondly, to what extent are spatial and visual memory organized into a modular system, with distinct modules for spatial and visual information.

Interest in the first question appears to have been stimulated by Hebb (1968) in a paper in which it was proposed that visuospatial memories are encoded as networks of associative links, which include a memory trace of both the visual information gathered during a fixation, and the eye movement vector for the subsequent fixation. In this view, activation of a visual image produces activation in the associated saccade vector, which then activates the relate visual images. This idea developed into scanpath theory, which held that visuo-spatial imagery required the activation or "reinstatement" of the sequence of eye movements (the scan path) used to encode the memoranda. Initially the evidence seemed consistent with this view, with the demonstration that eye movements during recall were highly correlated with eye movements during encoding (e.g. Noton & Stark, 1971), and that participants make saccades to empty spatial locations when recalling the objects that had been presented there (Ferreira, Apel & Henderson, 2008). However, since the 2010s this theory has fallen out of favor as evidence emerged that the eye movements during recall appeared to have no functional value, the most striking evidence of this being that re-instatement of a participant's own eye movements provided no benefit compared to reinstatement of someone else's eye movements (Foulsham & Kingstone, 2013). The prevailing view is now that, in the case of imagery, oculomotor activity is driven by the visual properties of the image, rather than oculomotor activity driving the construction of the image.

While some scholars focused on the mechanism for encoding spatial relations in episodic memory, others focused on the architecture of short-term memory,

DOI: 10.4324/9781003360896-6

attempting to use the dissociation technique to understand how memory could be fractionated into discrete cognitive modules. Using this technique, Baddeley and Hitch (Baddeley & Hitch, 1974) proposed that VSSTM comprised two passive, modular stores- a phonological store for verbal information and a spatial store for visuospatial information. They further argued that information in the phonological store could be kept active with a rehearsal mechanism called the phonological loop, which activated the verbal material to remembered. The rehearsal mechanism for the visuospatial store was not specified but, drawing on Hebb's proposal that motor traces act as associative links between visual snapshots acquired during encoding, Baddeley speculated it might take the form of an "oculomotor loop" which activated spatial locations in the form of eye movement vectors corresponding to the spatial location of visual memoranda. Consistent with this idea, Baddeley and others showed that eye movements during the maintenance of spatial information significantly reduced visuospatial memory span (Postle, Idzikowski, Della Sala, Logie & Baddeley, 2006). As it became clear that visual and spatial information were processed in distinct dorsal and ventral pathways (e.g. (Milner & Goodale, 1993; Mishkin, Ungerleider & Macko, 1983), the model was updated to include separate stores for visual and spatial information (Courtney, Petit, Maisog, Ungerleider & Haxby, 1998; Della Sala, Gray, Baddeley, Allamano & Wilson, 1999; Logie & Marchetti, 1991; Tresch, Sinnamon & Seamon, 1993), and it has subsequently been argued that the "oculomotor loop" plays a specific role in the maintenance of spatial information, but not non-spatial visual information in VSSTM (Ball, Pearson & Smith, 2013; Smith, 2022; Smith, Casteau & Archibald, 2021; McAteer, McGregor & Smith 2023).

Studies of eye movements have also been informative about the nature of representation in short term memory. Capacity in VSSTM has been proposed to be around three to four "slots" (Luck & Vogel, 1997), but there are strong individual differences, with capacity ranging from one to six items in some cases (Cowan, 2001). One popular idea that accounts for these interindividual differences is that VSSTM is a finite but flexible resource that is distributed amongst memoranda (Bays, 2015). According to this hypothesis, VSSTM capacity is not fixed but there is variability in the precision with which items can be retained, which can be measured by the continuous report task. This task requires participants to report a remembered feature along a continuous dimension, such as reporting the remembered color on a color wheel. Variability in precision depends on different task parameters such as memory load (Ma et al., 2014) and reflects differences in the distribution of memory resources across different items. There remains considerable debate about whether "slot" or "resource" models best capture the nature of VSSTM and one approach has been to model oculomotor behavior to try and arbitrate between the theories. For example Veksler et al. (2017), examined eye movements in a repeated serial search task, and reported that the recency and frequency of fixating targets improved their representation in memory. Comparison of the slot and resource memory models showed that the resource model provided the best fit to the data, taking account for the effects of how recently a target was fixated and the frequency with which it was fixated. However, while these findings illustrate how studies of oculomotor can be informative about the nature of representations in VSSTM, more work is needed to uncover precisely how the oculomotor system contributes to the precision of VSSTM.

This brief review demonstrates the important role studies using eye movements have played in understanding the cognitive mechanisms responsible for visuospatial STM. However, the precise functional role of the oculomotor system at different stages of VSSTM processing remains debated. There are several possibilities. Firstly, it is possible that the oculomotor system is primarily involved in the encoding locations of spatial locations. Eye movements are known to be preceded by a mandatory shift of attention and it is possible that the functional role of the oculomotor system is simply to ensure that gazed-at locations are attended and therefore encoded into STM. However, as we have seen, saccadic eye movements during maintenance also disrupt memory, consistent with a role for the oculomotor system in the maintenance as well as encoding of spatial locations. Finally, it is logically possible that activation of the oculomotor system is required for the recall of spatial information. The following sections review the evidence for these different functional roles.

2 Encoding

One possible role for the oculomotor system is that programming of eye movements facilitates the encoding of information at the saccade goal into spatial STM (sSTM; e.g. Van der Stigchel & Hollingworth, 2018). In a seminal study, Bays and Husain (2008) asked participants to remember either the orientation or spatial location of objects in multi-item displays and reported that the orientation and location of the saccade target was remembered more precisely than other items. This memory advantage for the saccade target was even observed if the saccade target was extinguished before the saccade landed on that item. Tas and colleagues (Tas, Luck & Hollingworth, 2016) subsequently showed that this automatic encoding of the target occurred only when participants were required to shift their attention overtly, but not when participants were asked to shift their attention covertly, Other studies have also demonstrated that saccades directed towards target locations or items bias entry into VSWM, resulting in a more precise representation of those objects and locations (Shao et al., 2010; Hanning, Jonikaitis, Deubel & Szinte, 2016; Ohl & Rolfs, 2017, 2020), and more recently, Udale, Tran, Manohar and Husain (2022) replicated and extended Bays and Husain (2008), proposing that saccade programming triggers the dynamic redistribution of resources away from stored memoranda to the upcoming saccade target on a moment-to-moment basis. The majority of studies therefore offer evidence in favor of the view that the oculomotor system plays a functional role in the encoding of information into VSWM, probably via the mandatory shift of attention that occurs prior to every eye movement (Deubel & Schneider, 1996; Shepherd, Findlay & Hockey, 1986).

Other scholars have reasoned that if the oculomotor system has a specific role in encoding memories, enforcing fixation during encoding should reduce memory performance. However, experiments that have compared memory on trials where eye movements are permitted during encoding with memory when fixation is enforced have produced somewhat mixed results. For example, it has been shown that saccades and on-item fixations during encoding can be beneficial, in that the number of fixations on task-relevant items and duration of these fixations during encoding was positively related to recall performance (Saint-Aubin, Tremblay & Jalbert, 2007). However, increasing fixation duration by slowing presentation rate did not improve recall performance for item order (Saint-Aubin et al., 2007). Furthermore, participants make few spontaneous on-item fixations when encoding under free viewing conditions, and these on-item fixations are not strongly related to spatial memory performance (Lange & Engbert, 2013; Patt et al., 2014; Souza, Czoschke & Lange, 2020). Martin and colleagues (Martin, Tapper, Gonzalez, Leclerc & Niechwiej-Szwedo, 2017) observed that enforcing central fixation during encoding elicited better performance than enforcing target-directed saccades for large set sizes (>7 items), but that at smaller set size the effect was in the opposite direction, perhaps indicating that set size is an important moderator of the functional role of the oculomotor system in sSTM. They speculate that making target directed when there are many items in a display disrupts other, complementary mnemonic processes such as chunking or the formation of configural images. In a related study Czoschke, Henschke and Lange (2019) report no difference in spatial span when participants were asked to maintain central fixation compared to when they freely view memoranda during the encoding phase. Together these studies suggest that fixating items during encoding has a limited impact on memory performance.

On first inspection it seems hard to reconcile Bays and others' observation that saccades reliably enhance memory for the saccade target with the finding that fixating objects does not reliably enhance memory. However, it is important to note "presaccadic" advantage is only observed for the *final* item in a sequence (Bayes & Husain, 2008, Udale et al., 2022), not all the items that were fixated. Given that the studies that correlate fixation with performance use many items, only one of which will benefit from the fixation, it is easier to reconcile the two sets of data, because the benefit of freely viewing memoranda will be relatively small when considered across all presented items. A further limitation of studies that comparing fixed and free viewing conditions is that they do not adequately disentangle the effects of oculomotor control processes from those of attentional processes, which are known to be tightly coupled (e.g. Casteau & Smith, 2019; Corbetta et al., 1998; Rizzolatti, Riggio & Sheliga, 1994; Smith & Schenk, 2012). It therefore remains possible that the oculomotor system was covertly activated in order to drive attention to memoranda, even when overt eye movements were prohibited. Pearson, Ball and Smith (2014) directly addressed this issue using the "eye abduction" technique (Craighero, Nascimben & Fadiga, 2004). Eye-abduction involves abduction of the dominant eye such that participants view the stimulus display angle of gaze in 40 degrees from the body and head midline, with the other eye patched. The rationale is that stimuli at eccentric locations can be seen but cannot be reached with a saccadic eye movement. This manipulation therefore disrupts saccade programming (Boon, Theeuwes & Belopolsky, 2017), and exogenous covert attention (Smith, Rorden & Schenk, 2012), but does not affect endogenous, covert orienting of attention (Casteau & Smith, 2020; Morgan, Ball & Smith, 2014; Smith, Ball & Ellison, 2014; Smith et al., 2012). Pearson and colleagues showed that when eye-abduction was applied during encoding phase of a serial spatial memory task (a modified Corsi blocks task) there was a small but significant reduction in spatial span when items appeared at locations that could not become the goal of a saccadic eye movement. Notably, memory for visual features such as orientation were not affected by the manipulation. Pearson and colleagues argued that under normal viewing conditions the visual transients associated with the appearance of memory items in the Corsi task activate saccade programs in the oculomotor system. This activation supports the encoding of the spatial locations of the memoranda in VSSTM. Eye abduction disrupts the automatic saccade programming, and therefore the encoding of spatial information into VSSTM. This explanation is consistent with the evidence that eye abduction results in disruption to the Corsi task, which uses sudden onsets, but not the arrow-span task, which uses symbolic cues to indicate the memorized location (Ball et al., 2013). Overall the data seem to suggest two related but partially dissociable functions for the oculomotor system during encoding. The work on presaccadic encoding suggests that one role is to improve the precision of representations via presaccadic shifts of attention that prioritize the encoding of information at the saccade goal with a high degree of precision (Bays & Husain, 2008; Udale et al., 2022; Ohl & Rolfs, 2017). In parallel, the studies of oculomotor disruption during encoding indicate that activation of oculomotor programs can support the optimal encoding of spatial locations indicated by visual transients.

3 Maintenance

Considerable research has been conducted examining the role of the oculomotor system in maintaining and rehearsing information in VSSTM. Two theoretical positions have largely dominated this debate. The attentional rehearsal view (Awh & Jonides, 2001; Awh, Jonides & Reuter-Lorenz, 1998) holds that maintenance and rehearsal in VSSTM is achieved using attentional "refreshing," during which covert attention is directed to different spatial locations in order to maintain their activation in memory. In this view, oculomotor activity during rehearsal is an epiphenomenon of close coupling between covert attention and oculomotor control. The contrasting view is that of the "oculomotor loop," which hypothesizes that maintenance spatial memory relies on the activation of saccade programs to the to-be-remembered locations in the oculomotor system (Baddeley, 1986; Postle et al., 2006). Given that the brain areas involved in VSSTM, covert attention and saccade control have considerable overlap (Ikkai & Curtis, 2011), differentiating these theoretical positions using neuroimaging approaches is problematic, and much of the focus of experimental work has been on ingenious behavioral experiments.

One approach has been to ask how holding something in memory affects orienting of attention. If the attentional rehearsal hypothesis is correct, and covert shifts in attention to memorized locations are the primary rehearsal mechanism in VSSTM (Awh & Jonides, 2001; Awh et al., 1998) covert attention should be directed to the locations held in VSSTM. Consistent with this prediction, Awh et al. (1998) showed that when a location is held in VSSTM, perceptual processing is enhanced at that location. They further showed that spatial working memory performance was disrupted when attention was shifted to non-memorized locations during the delay period, suggesting that attention was directed towards locations held in VSSTM during the maintenance period. Indeed, a considerable body of other evidence also suggests that holding a location in VSSTM leads to attentional prioritization of that location (Olivers, Peters, Houtkamp & Roelfsema, 2011). Following similar logic, it has been argued that if the oculomotor system also has an important functional role in the maintenance of spatial memories, one might expect to a correlation between delay-period fixations on memorized locations and accuracy of recall. Consistent with this prediction, Tremblay, Saint-Aubin and Jalbert (2006) reported a positive correlation between the number of fixations towards a pair of serially presented to-be-remembered locations and spatial memory performance has been observed. Similarly, Olsen, Chiew, Buchsbaum and Ryan (2014) showed that the degree of similarity between eye movements performed at encoding and eye movements during the retention interval predicts memory performance, but only when information about relative spatial locations was available during recall. Lilienthal, Myerson, Abrams and Hale (2018) also report that overt rehearsal leads to enhanced memory span, with rehearsal interval fixations on memorized locations predicting memory performance. However, these findings are not without their limitations. Specifically, in Tremblay et al.'s (2006) study, participants fixated at least one pair of locations on only around two thirds of trials. This suggests that maintenance period eye movements might make a relatively minor contribution to rehearsal in VSWM. More problematically, in some studies the stimulus array remained on screen during the maintenance period, and this "environmental support" for rehearsal has been shown to influence both memory performance and delay-period oculomotor activity (Lilienthal et al., 2018; Souza et al., 2020). Indeed, Godijn and Theeuwes (2012) carried out a similar study to Tremblay et al. (2006) in which participants were asked to either freely view or maintain fixation on a single point during the delay-period of a spatial serial recall task. In this case no difference in memory performance was found between free and fixed viewing conditions, indicating that in the absence of a stimulus array, delay-period eye movements are not functional, but are a reflection of covert attentional rehearsal in VSSTM (see also Souza et al., 2020; Olsen et al. 2014, experiment 2; Lilienthal et al., 2018).

An alternative approach has been to study the effects of holding a location in STM on the metrics of saccadic eye movements. Using this approach,

Theeuwes, Olivers and Chizk (2005), have shown that holding a location in memory causes saccade trajectories to deviate away from that spatial location. Similarly, holding a location in VSSTM retards the latency of saccades directed to that location, and this oculomotor inhibition is associated with reduced perceptual accuracy (Belopolsky & Theeuwes, 2009a, 2009b, 2011; Ostendorf, Finke & Ploner, 2004). Given that deviations in saccade trajectories are driven by activation at the level of the superior colliculus, these studies seem to suggest that the oculomotor system plays an important functional role in the maintenance of spatial representations. This is also evidenced by the reduced accuracy usually reported when participants are asked to make a saccades directed towards a previously memorized location (or *memory-guided* saccades), as they generally tend to be more hypometric compared to visually guided saccades (Gnadt, Bracewell & Andersen, 1991; Nuthmann, Vitu, Engbert & Kliegl, 2016). For example, Herwig and colleagues (Herwig, Beisert & Schneider, 2010) studied the effect of an irrelevant distractor on memory-guided saccades and observed that saccades tended to deviate towards an intermediate location between the two stimuli. This effect mimicked the well-known saccade averaging effect (or global effect; Findlay, 1982) and seem to suggest that eye movement control and VSSTM rely on the same spatial maps.

Saccadic interference studies, in which participants make eye movements to irrelevant locations during the maintenance period (Lawrence, Myerson & Abrams, 2004; Pearson & Sahraie, 2003; Peterson, Kelly & Blumberg, 2019; Postle et al., 2006) also suggest a tight coupling between oculomotor control and the maintenance of VSSTM. A notable example of this comes from Pearson and Sahraie (2003). Using a selective interference paradigm, they compared different types of interference performed during the retention interval of the Corsi blocks task, including saccadic interference, limb movement and covert attentional interference. They showed that saccades performed during the retention interval disrupted spatial span significantly more than other interference conditions, including covert shifts of attention and other spatially guide actions such as pointing. Subsequent studies comparing the effect of saccadic interference on phonological and spatial memory (Lawrence et al., 2004) and color and spatial memory (McAteer et al., 2023) have shown the disruptive effect of saccades is specific to the maintenance of spatial information in VSSTM. Together, these data appear consistent with the claim that the oculomotor system and attention systems make distinct and dissociable contributions to the maintenance of spatial information, but that the oculomotor system is much less important for the maintenance of nonspatial information.

The skeptical reader might object that making saccadic eye movements necessarily involve shifts of attention (Deubel & Schneider, 1996; Shepherd et al., 1986), so studies that use saccadic interference cannot truly demonstrate a specific role for the oculomotor system in the maintenance of spatial WM. To clarify the extent to which oculomotor system contributes to maintenance independently of attentional control processes, Pearson et al. (2014) applied eye-abduction (Craighero et al., 2004) during STM tasks. Pearson and colleagues demonstrated that application of eye-abduction, and therefore the disruption of saccadic programming, during the retention interval significantly disrupted spatial span on the Corsi blocks task but not the visual patterns task. As noted above, the same manipulation does not reliably disrupt endogenous covert attention, demonstrating that the oculomotor system has a role in the maintenance of VSSTM that is dissociable from the role of covert orienting of attention.

To summarize, there is extensive evidence that both oculomotor and attentional processes are active during maintenance of spatial short-term memories. Correlational approaches such as neuroimaging and scanpath measurement cannot reliably differentiate between attentional and oculomotor processes, but dual tasks studies of the effect on maintenance on saccade metrics, interference tasks such as delay-period saccades and eye-abduction demonstrate that the oculomotor system make a specific, functional contribution to the maintenance of spatial locations in STM that is independent of the role of attentional rehearsal.

4 Retrieval

A final possibility is that the oculomotor system may be involved in aiding short term memory retrieval. Indeed, the scanpath theory (Noton & Stark, 1971) introduced above proposed that recreating the complete sequence of saccades from encoding facilitated retrieval. The "looking at nothing" phenomenon, in which gaze, but not necessarily the sequence of saccades, is directed towards locations held in memory to facilitate the recall of information that was previously presented at that location, has been observed in visual mental imagery tasks, visual long-term memory tasks, and in verbal memory tasks (Brandt & Stark, 1997; Ferreira et al., 2008; Spivey & Geng, 2001). In the same vein, some studies have argued that the degree of overlap in fixations between encoding and retrieval is positively correlated with memory accuracy in verbal (Richardson & Spivey, 2000) and visuospatial (Olsen et al., 2014; Wynn, Shen & Ryan, 2019) memory tasks. Indeed, Johansson, Holsanova, Dewhurst and Holmqvist (2012) showed that maintaining fixation during encoding did not affect oculomotor activity during retrieval whereas maintaining fixation during *retrieval* disrupted memory performance. Additionally, it has been shown that false alarm rates in memory are significantly higher when eye movements are restricted during recall (Damiano & Walther, 2019), which has been taken as evidence that oculomotor activity is functional for memory retrieval.

However, this functional role of oculomotor activation at retrieval is disputed. For example Martarelli and Mast (2013) reported that memory accuracy was not increased when gaze was directed to locations where stimuli had appeared compared to locations that were not relevant. Similarly, while spontaneously re-visiting encoded locations produced a beneficial effect at recall, there was no advantage to re-tracing the *exact* scanpath (Foulsham & Kingstone, 2013. Indeed, others have convincingly argued that the oculomotor activity is a reflection of attention shifts towards memoranda at recall (Scholz, Klichowicz & Krems, 2018; van Ede, Chekroud & Nobre, 2019). Kinjo et al. (2020) also examined the function and characteristics of eye movements in VSWM for visual images and locations by manipulating viewing conditions. The "looking at nothing" phenomenon was observed in free viewing conditions, where gaze was shifted towards the location associated with the visual object, but there was no difference in memory performance between free and fixed viewing conditions. These results appear to suggest that eye movements do not play a functional role in VSWM retrieval. Kinjo et al. (2020) also considered whether microsaccades during fixed viewing may play a role in retrieval. No evidence that microsaccades were directed towards associated locations during retrieval was observed, consistent with the view that microsaccades during rehearsal reflect the allocation of covert spatial attention (van Ede et al., 2019), though direct comparisons between these studies are difficult due to the different natures of the tasks involved. Other studies looking specifically at short-term memory also suggest that the oculomotor system plays a limited role in short-term memory retrieval. For example, when eye-abduction is applied during recall there is no effect on Corsi span (Ball et al., 2013) and Masson et al. (2021) report the interesting case of a patient who suffers congenital horizontal gaze palsy. If the oculomotor system is involved in the recall of spatial STM, then one might expect poorer recall when the memoranda appear at locations along the paralyzed axis compared to the axis along which eye movements are preserved. However, this was not the case; the location of the stimuli made no difference patient's ability to use a retro-cue guide recall in a delayed match-to-sample task for orientation, consistent with other evidence that the oculomotor system plays a very limited role in the recall of visual features.

To summarize, there is continued debate about whether the oculomotor system has a functional role in the retrieval of information from VSWM, and if so, what this role is. Some argue that spatial locations act as a retrieval cue to which other information is bound (Johansson & Johansson, 2014). Others argue that eye movements are epiphenomenal to covert shifts of attention during recall (Scholz et al., 2018), but on balance the behavioral and neuropsychological evidence is more consistent with the view that the oculomotor system plays a limited role in recall of visuospatial information.

5 A functional role of the oculomotor system in spatial STM

There is a significant body of behavioral, neurophysiological, neuropsychological and neuroimaging evidence demonstrating a functional overlap between the oculomotor system and VSSTM, especially in the encoding and maintenance of information in VSSTM. This functional overlap appears to derive from two sources. Firstly, making saccadic eye movements involves presaccadic shifts of attention which lead to the mandatory encoding of the saccade target into spatial STM with a high degree of precision. Secondly, spatial locations appear to be represented in the spatial maps used by oculomotor system during the maintenance of spatial information. This latter role for the oculomotor system is consistent with models of spatial STM that invoke a hypothetical "priority map" to explain spatial STM (e.g., Ikkai & Curtis, 2011; Zelinsky & Bisley,

2015). In this view VSWM is encoded and maintained in a "priority map" that is also used to control visually guided action. This map integrates bottom-up signals about the physical salience of different locations with top-down signal relating to the task-relevance of the locations. Salient and/or important locations are represented at peaks of activation (Bisley & Goldberg, 2010; Fecteau & Munoz, 2006), and these peaks can be "read-out" by the visual system to guide attention or by the oculomotor system to guide eye movements. Critically, activity in the map is sustained once stimuli have disappeared (Ikkai & Curtis 2011) and can therefore maintain representations of behaviorally relevant spatial locations. Recursive feedback loops between the priority map and oculomotor system allow activation relating to saccade plans in the oculomotor system to influence activity levels in the priority map (Barash, Bracewell, Fogassi, Gnadt & Andersen, 1991), allowing prioritizing of representations of saccade targets and accounting for the ability of memorized locations to affect saccade metrics. Spatial short term memories can therefore be conceptualized as activation peaks in the priority map, whose activation can be sustained by covertly attending to these locations (Awh et al., 1998; Godijn & Theeuwes, 2012; Postle et al., 2006; Scholz et al., 2018), by planning eye movements to those locations (Ball, Pearson & Smith, 2013; Pearson et al., 2014) or by overtly fixating them (Lilienthal et al., 2018; Tremblay et al., 2006). Delay period saccades to task-irrelevant locations, lead to (a) the mandatory encoding of saccade targets into memory, which effectively increases the set-size, thus making the task harder and leading to an apparently decreased span in the Corsi task and (b) the noisy updating of the spatial maps used maintain spatial locations. Consistent with this interpretation, delay period saccades lead to increased guessing (McAteer et al., 2023) and decreased precision (Peterson et al., 2019) of VSSTM representations. Attentional interference is less disruptive because shifts of attention don't produce the mandatory encoding of the attended location to STM or require updating of spatial maps. Disruption to the oculomotor system by eye-abduction or in neurological disease (Smith & Archibald, 2020) interferes with the recursive links between the parietal structures that encode the priority map and basal ganglia structures that encode eye movements. This disruption reduces the potential for activity in the oculomotor system to contribute to the maintenance of activation peaks in the priority map during delay periods. This manifests as reduced span in Corsi-style tasks, and increased imprecision and guessing in continuous report tasks. This dual role account of the oculomotor system in VSSTM accounts for the majority of existing evidence and points to several lines of future enquiry. For example, if VSSTM and saccade control draw on the same spatial map, manipulations such as saccadic adaptation should lead to disrupted sSTM as the priority map and oculomotor maps become misaligned. Similarly, it should be possible to observe reliable associations between oculomotor dysfunction and VSSTM, which is specific to the spatial component of STM and these associations may have practical utility for the early and more accurate diagnosis of some neurological diseases. Another open question is the extent to which activation of the priority map guides other actions, such as pointing or reaching and grasping. One possibility is the action preparation in these modalities also influences maintenance in the priority map (note that limb movements do cause reduction in span), which would certainly be consistent with the evidence that all spatially directed actions have some disruptive effect on memory, albeit not as severe as that of eye movements (Pearson & Sahraie, 2003). In this case, it may be predicted that any goal directed action should produce mandatory encoding of the target object in VSWM (Casteau et al., unpublished data).

6 Conclusion

The role of the eye movement system in spatial short-term memory has been the subject of extensive research over the past 40 years. While a strict interpretation of Hebb's original proposal that saccade vectors act as retrieval cues that permit the reconstruction of visuospatial representations has not withstood empirical test, the central insight that oculomotor activity has a profound impact on cognitive processes has survived, albeit in modified form. More specifically, the evidence seems to point to a role for the oculomotor system in the presaccadic encoding of visual features and spatial information and highly specialized functional role in the maintenance of spatial STM which does not extend to maintenance of non-spatial features such as color. In contrast, retrieval from sSTM appears much less tightly coupled to the oculomotor system than encoding or maintenance. This proposition is consistent with neurophysiological models which hypothesize that sSTM is coded as activation in a feature-free spatial priority map which emerges from recursive links between parietal brain regions which encode space and subcortical areas that drive saccadic eye movements. Moving forward, a key issue to address will how these theoretical insights might be translated into applications, for example in the early or more accurate diagnosis of neurological disease.

References

Awh, E. & Jonides, J. (2001). Overlapping mechanisms of attention and spatial working memory. *Trends in Cognitive Sciences*, 5(3), 119–126. doi:10.1016/s1364-6613(00)01593-x.

Awh, E., Jonides, J. & Reuter-Lorenz, P. A. (1998). Rehearsal in spatial working memory. *Journal of Experimental Psychology-Human Perception and Performance*, 24 (3), 780–790. doi:10.1037//0096-1523.24.3.780.

Baddeley, A. D. (1986). *Working memory*. Oxford University Press.

Baddeley, A. D. & Hitch, G. (1974). Working memory. In G. H. Bower (Ed.), *Psychology of learning and motivation* (vol. 8, pp. 47–89): Academic Press.

Ball, K., Pearson, D. G. & Smith, D. T. (2013). Oculomotor involvement in spatial working memory is task-specific. *Cognition*, 129(2), 439–446. doi:10.1016/j.cognition.2013.08.006.

Barash, S., Bracewell, R. M., Fogassi, L., Gnadt, J. W. & Andersen, R. A. (1991). Saccade-related activity in the lateral intraparietal area. I. Temporal properties; comparison with area 7a. *J Neurophysiol*, 66(3), 1095–1108. doi:10.1152/jn.1991.66.3.1095.

Bays, P. M. (2015). Spikes not slots: noise in neural populations limits working memory. *Trends in Cognitive Sciences*, 19(8), 431–438. doi:10.1016/j.tics.2015.06.004.

Bays, P. M. & Husain, M. (2008). Dynamic shifts of limited working memory resources in human vision. *Science*, 321(5890), 851–854. doi:10.1126/science.1158023.

Belopolsky, A. V. & Theeuwes, J. (2009a). Inhibition of saccadic eye movements to locations in spatial working memory. *Attention Perception & Psychophysics*, 71(3), 620–631. doi:10.3758/app.71.3.620.

Belopolsky, A. V. & Theeuwes, J. (2009b). No functional role of attention-based rehearsal in maintenance of spatial working memory representations. *Acta Psychologica*, 132(2), 124–135. doi:10.1016/j.actpsy.2009.01.002.

Belopolsky, A. V. & Theeuwes, J. (2011). Selection within visual memory representations activates the oculomotor system. *Neuropsychologia*, 49(6), 1605–1610. doi:10.1016/j.neuropsychologia.2010.12.045.

Bisley, J. W. & Goldberg, M. E. (2010). Attention, intention, and priority in the parietal lobe. *Annual Review of Neuroscience*, 33(1), 1–21. doi:10.1146/annurev-neuro-060909-152823.

Boon, P. J., Theeuwes, J. & Belopolsky, A. V. (2017). Eye abduction reduces but does not eliminate competition in the oculomotor system. *Journal of Vision*, 17(5), 15–15. doi:10.1167/17.5.15.

Brandt, S. A. & Stark, L. W. (1997). Spontaneous eye movements during visual imagery reflect the content of the visual scene. *Journal of Cognitive Neuroscience*, 9(1), 27–38. doi:10.1162/jocn.1997.9.1.27.

Casteau, S. & Smith, D. T. (2019). Associations and dissociations between oculomotor readiness and covert attention. *Vision*, 3(2), 17.

Casteau, S. & Smith, D. T. (2020). Covert attention beyond the range of eye movements: Evidence for a dissociation between exogenous and endogenous orienting. *Cortex*, 122, 170–186. doi:10.1016/j.cortex.2018.11.007.

Corbetta, M., Akbudak, E., Conturo, T. E., Snyder, A. Z., Ollinger, J. M., Drury, H. A., ... Shulman, G. L. (1998). A common network of functional areas for attention and eye movements. *Neuron*, 21(4), 761–773.

Courtney, S. M., Petit, L., Maisog, J. M., Ungerleider, L. G. & Haxby, J. V. (1998). An area specialized for spatial working memory in human frontal cortex. *Science*, 279 (5355), 1347–1351. doi:doi:10.1126/science.279.5355.1347.

Cowan, N. (2001). The magical number 4 in short-term memory: A reconsideration of mental storage capacity. *Behavioral and Brain Sciences*, 24(1), 87–114. doi:10.1017/S0140525X01003922.

Craighero, L., Nascimben, M. & Fadiga, L. (2004). Eye position affects orienting of visuospatial attention. *Current Biology*, 14(4), 331–333.

Czoschke, S., Henschke, S. & Lange, E. (2019). On-item fixations during serial encoding do not affect spatial working memory. *Attention, Perception & Psychophysics*, 81. doi:10.3758/s13414-019-01786-5.

Damiano, C. & Walther, D. B. (2019). Distinct roles of eye movements during memory encoding and retrieval. *Cognition*, 184, 119–129. doi:10.1016/j.cognition.2018.12.014.

Della Sala, S., Gray, C., Baddeley, A., Allamano, N. & Wilson, L. (1999). Pattern span: a tool for unwelding visuo–spatial memory. *Neuropsychologia*, 37(10), 1189–1199. doi:10.1016/S0028-3932(98)00159-6.

Deubel, H. & Schneider, W. X. (1996). Saccade target selection and object recognition: Evidence for a common attentional mechanism. *Vision Research*, 36(12), 1827–1837.

Fecteau, J. H. & Munoz, D. P. (2006). Salience, relevance, and firing: a priority map for target selection. *Trends in Cognitive Sciences*, 10(8), 382–390.

Ferreira, F., Apel, J. & Henderson, J. M. (2008). Taking a new look at looking at nothing. *Trends in Cognitive Sciences*, 12(11), 405–410. doi:10.1016/j.tics.2008.07.007.

Findlay, J. M. (1982). Global visual processing for saccadic eye movements. *Vision Res*, 22(8), 1033–1045. doi:10.1016/0042-6989(82)90040-2.

Findlay, J. M. & Gilchrist, I. D. (2003). *Active vision: The psychology of looking and seeing*. Oxford University Press.

Foulsham, T. & Kingstone, A. (2013). Fixation-dependent memory for natural scenes: an experimental test of scanpath theory. *J Exp Psychol Gen*, 142(1), 41–56. doi:10.1037/a0028227.

Gnadt, J. W., Bracewell, R. M. & Andersen, R. A. (1991). Sensorimotor transformation during eye movements to remembered visual targets. *Vision Res*, 31(4), 693–715.

Godijn, R. & Theeuwes, J. (2012). Overt is no better than covert when rehearsing visuo-spatial information in working memory. *Memory & Cognition*, 40(1), 52–61. doi:10.3758/s13421-011-0132-x.

Hanning, N. M., Jonikaitis, D., Deubel, H. & Szinte, M. (2016). Oculomotor selection underlies feature retention in visual working memory. *Journal of Neurophysiology*, 115(2), 1071–1076. doi:10.1152/jn.00927.2015.

Hebb, D. O. (1968). Concerning imagery. *Psychological Review*, 75(6), 466–477. doi:10.1037/h0026771.

Herwig, A., Beisert, M. & Schneider, W. X. (2010). On the spatial interaction of visual working memory and attention: evidence for a global effect from memory-guided saccades. *J Vis*, 10(5), 8. doi:10.1167/10.5.8.

Ikkai, A. & Curtis, C. E. (2011). Common neural mechanisms supporting spatial working memory, attention and motor intention. *Neuropsychologia*, 49(6), 1428–1434.

Johansson, R., Holsanova, J., Dewhurst, R. & Holmqvist, K. (2012). Eye movements during scene recollection have a functional role, but they are not reinstatements of those produced during encoding. *Journal of Experimental Psychology: Human Perception and Performance*, 38(5), 1289–1314. doi:10.1037/a0026585.

Johansson, R. & Johansson, M. (2014). Look here, eye movements play a functional role in memory retrieval. *Psychological Science*, 25(1), 236–242.

Kinjo, H., Fooken, J. & Spering, M. (2020). Do eye movements enhance visual memory retrieval?. *Vision Research*, 176, 80–90.

Lange, E. B. & Engbert, R. (2013). Differentiating between verbal and spatial encoding using eye movement recordings. *Q J Exp Psychol (Hove)*, 66(9), 1840–1857. doi:10.1080/17470218.2013.772214.

Lawrence, B. M., Myerson, J. & Abrams, R. A. (2004). Interference with spatial working memory: An eye movement is more than a shift of attention. *Psychonomic Bulletin & Review*, 11(3), 488–494. doi:10.3758/BF03196600.

Lilienthal, L., Myerson, J., Abrams, R. A. & Hale, S. (2018). Effects of environmental support on overt and covert visuospatial rehearsal. *Memory*, 1–11. doi:10.1080/09658211.2018.1462390.

Logie, R. H. & Marchetti, C. (1991). Visuo-spatial working memory: Visual, spatial or central executive? In R. H. Logie & M. Denis (Eds.), *Advances in psychology* (vol. 80, pp. 105–115): North-Holland.

Luck, S. J. & Vogel, E. K. (1997). The capacity of visual working memory for features and conjunctions. *Nature*, 390(6657), 279–281.

Ma, W. J., Husain, M. & Bays, P. M. (2014). Changing concepts of working memory. *Nature Neuroscience*, 17(3), 347–356.

Martarelli, C. S. & Mast, F. W. (2013). Eye movements during long-term pictorial recall. *Psychological Research-Psychologische Forschung*, 77(3), 303–309. doi:10.1007/s00426-012-0439-7.

Martin, L., Tapper, A., Gonzalez, D. A., Leclerc, M. & Niechwiej-Szwedo, E. (2017). The effects of task-relevant saccadic eye movements performed during the encoding of a serial sequence on visuospatial memory performance. *Experimental Brain Research*, 235(5), 1519–1529. doi:10.1007/s00221-017-4915-6.

Masson, N., Andres, M., Carneiro Pereira, S., Vandenberghe, A., Pesenti, M. & Vannuscorps, G. (2021). Shifting attention in visuospatial short-term memory does not require oculomotor planning: Insight from congenital gaze paralysis. *Neuropsychologia*, 161, 107998. doi:10.1016/j.neuropsychologia.2021.107998.

McAteer, S. M., McGregor, A. & Smith, D. T. (2023). Oculomotor rehearsal in visuospatial working memory. *Attention, Perception & Psychophysics*, 85(1), 261–275.

Milner, A. D. & Goodale, M. A. (1993). Visual pathways to perception and action. *Progress in Brain Research*, 95, 317–337.

Mishkin, M., Ungerleider, L. G. & Macko, K. A. (1983). Object vision and spatial vision: two cortical pathways. *Trends in Neurosciences*, 6, 414–417.

Morgan, E. J., Ball, K. & Smith, D. T. (2014). The role of the oculomotor system in covert social attention. *Attention Perception & Psychophysics*, 76(5), 1265–1270. doi:10.3758/s13414-014-0716-1.

Noton, D. & Stark, L. (1971). Scanpaths in eye movements during pattern perception. *Science*, 171(3968), 308–311. doi:10.1126/science.171.3968.308.

Nuthmann, A., Vitu, F., Engbert, R. & Kliegl, R. (2016). No evidence for a saccadic range effect for visually guided and memory-guided saccades in simple saccade-targeting tasks. *PLoS One*, 11(9), e0162449. doi:10.1371/journal.pone.0162449.

Ohl, S. & Rolfs, M. (2017). Saccadic eye movements impose a natural bottleneck on visual short-term memory. *J Exp Psychol Learn Mem Cogn*, 43(5), 736–748. doi:10.1037/xlm0000338.

Ohl, S. & Rolfs, M. (2020). Bold moves: Inevitable saccadic selection in visual short-term memory. *Journal of Vision*, 20(2), 11–11. doi:10.1167/jov.20.2.11.

Olivers, C. N. L., Peters, J., Houtkamp, R. & Roelfsema, P. R. (2011). Different states in visual working memory: when it guides attention and when it does not. *Trends in Cognitive Sciences*, 15(7), 327–334.

Olsen, R. K., Chiew, M., Buchsbaum, B. R. & Ryan, J. D. (2014). The relationship between delay period eye movements and visuospatial memory. *Journal of Vision*, 14 (1), 8–8. doi:10.1167/14.1.8.

Ostendorf, F., Finke, C. & Ploner, C. J. (2004). Inhibition of visual discrimination during a memory-guided saccade task. *Journal of Neurophysiology*, 92(1), 660–664. doi:10.1152/jn.01045.2003.

Patt, V. M., Thomas, M. L., Minassian, A., Geyer, M. A., Brown, G. G. & Perry, W. (2014). Disentangling working memory processes during spatial span assessment: A modeling analysis of preferred eye movement strategies. *Journal of Clinical and Experimental Neuropsychology*, 36(2), 186–204. doi:10.1080/13803395.2013.877123.

Pearson, D. G., Ball, K. & Smith, D. T. (2014). Oculomotor preparation as a rehearsal mechanism in spatial working memory. *Cognition*, 132(3), 416–428. doi:10.1016/j.cognition.2014.05.006.

Pearson, D. G. & Sahraie, A. (2003). Oculomotor control and the maintenance of spatially and temporally distributed events in visuo-spatial working memory. *Quarterly*

Journal of Experimental Psychology Section a-Human Experimental Psychology, 56 (7), 1089–1111. doi:10.1080/02724980343000044.

Peterson, M. S., Kelly, S. P. & Blumberg, E. J. (2019). Saccadic eye movements smear spatial working memory. *Journal of Experimental Psychology: Human Perception and Performance*, 45(2), 255–263. doi:10.1037/xhp0000596.

Postle, B. R., Idzikowski, C., Della Sala, S., Logie, R. H. & Baddeley, A. D. (2006). The selective disruption of spatial working memory by eye movements. *Quarterly Journal of Experimental Psychology*, 59(1), 100–120. doi:10.1080/17470210500151410.

Richardson, D. C. & Spivey, M. J. (2000). Representation, space and Hollywood Squares: looking at things that aren't there anymore. *Cognition*, 76(3), 269–295. doi:10.1016/s0010-0277(00)00084-6.

Rizzolatti, G., Riggio, L. & Sheliga, B. M. (1994). Space and selective attention. *Attention and Performance*, 15, 231–265.

Saint-Aubin, J., Tremblay, S. & Jalbert, A. (2007). Eye movements and serial memory for visual-spatial information: does time spent fixating contribute to recall? *Exp Psychol*, 54(4), 264–272. doi:10.1027/1618-3169.54.4.264.

Scholz, A., Klichowicz, A. & Krems, J. F. (2018). Covert shifts of attention can account for the functional role of "eye movements to nothing". *Memory & Cognition*, 46(2), 230–243. doi:10.3758/s13421-017-0760-x.

Shao, N., Li, J., Shui, R., Zheng, X., Lu, J. & Shen, M. (2010). Saccades elicit obligatory allocation of visual working memory. *Memory & Cognition*, 38(5), 629–640.

Shepherd, M., Findlay, J. M. & Hockey, R. J. (1986). The relationship between eye movements and spatial attention. *Quarterly Journal of Experimental Psychology Section a-Human Experimental Psychology*, 38(3), 475–491.

Smith, D. T. (2022). A horizontal–vertical anisotropy in spatial short-term memory. *Visual Cognition*, 1–9. doi:10.1080/13506285.2022.2042446.

Smith, D. T. & Archibald, N. (2020). Spatial working memory in progressive supranuclear palsy. *Cortex*, 122, 115–122. doi:10.1016/j.cortex.2018.07.004.

Smith, D. T., Ball, K. & Ellison, A. (2014). Covert visual search within and beyond the effective oculomotor range. *Vision Research*, 95, 11–17. doi:10.1016/j.visres.2013.12.003.

Smith, D. T., Casteau, S. & Archibald, N. (2021). Spatial attention and spatial short term memory in PSP and Parkinson's disease. *Cortex*, 137, 49–60. doi:10.1016/j.cortex.2020.12.019.

Smith, D. T., Rorden, C. & Schenk, T. (2012). Saccade preparation is required for exogenous attention but not endogenous attention or IOR. *Journal of Experimental Psychology-Human Perception and Performance*, 36(6), 1438–1447. doi:10.1037/a0027794.

Smith, D. T. & Schenk, T. (2012). The premotor theory of attention: Time to move on? *Neuropsychologia*, 50(6), 1104–1114.

Souza, A. S., Czoschke, S. & Lange, E. B. (2020). Gaze-based and attention-based rehearsal in spatial working memory. *Journal of Experimental Psychology-Learning Memory and Cognition*, 46(5), 980–1003. doi:10.1037/xlm0000771.

Spivey, M. J. & Geng, J. J. (2001). Oculomotor mechanisms activated by imagery and memory: eye movements to absent objects. *Psychological Research-Psychologische Forschung*, 65(4), 235–241. doi:10.1007/s004260100059.

Tas, A. C., Luck, S. J. & Hollingworth, A. (2016). The relationship between visual attention and visual working memory encoding: A dissociation between covert and overt orienting. *Journal of experimental psychology: human perception and performance*, 42(8), 1121.

Theeuwes, J., Olivers, C. N. L. & Chizk, C. L. (2005). Remembering a location makes the eyes curve away. *Psychological Science*, 16(3), 196–199. doi:10.1111/j.0956-7976.2005.00803.x.
Tremblay, S., Saint-Aubin, J. & Jalbert, A. (2006). Rehearsal in serial memory for visual-spatial information: evidence from eye movements. *Psychon Bull Rev*, 13(3), 452–457.
Tresch, M. C., Sinnamon, H. M. & Seamon, J. G. (1993). Double dissociation of spatial and object visual memory: Evidence from selective interference in intact human subjects. *Neuropsychologia*, 31(3), 211–219. https://doi.org/10.1016/0028-3932(93)90085-E.
Udale, R., Tran, M. T., Manohar, S. & Husain, M. (2022). Dynamic in-flight shifts of working memory resources across saccades. *Journal of Experimental Psychology: Human Perception and Performance*, 48, 21–36. doi:10.1037/xhp0000960.
Van der Stigchel, S. & Hollingworth, A. (2018). Visuospatial Working Memory as a Fundamental Component of the Eye Movement System. *Current Directions in Psychological Science*, 27(2), 136–143. doi:10.1177/0963721417741710.
van Ede, F., Chekroud, S. R. & Nobre, A. C. (2019). Human gaze tracks attentional focusing in memorized visual space. *Nature human behaviour*, 3(5), 462–470. doi:10.1038/s41562-019-0549-y.
Veksler, B. Z., Boyd, R., Myers, C. W., Gunzelmann, G., Neth, H. & Gray, W. D. (2017). Visual working memory resources are best characterized as dynamic, quantifiable mnemonic traces. *Topics in Cognitive Science*, 9(1), 83–101.
Wynn, J. S., Shen, K. & Ryan, J. D. (2019). Eye Movements Actively Reinstate Spatiotemporal Mnemonic Content. *Vision*, 3(2), 21.
Zelinsky, G. J. & Bisley, J. W. (2015). The what, where, and why of priority maps and their interactions with visual working memory. *Annals of the New York Academy of Sciences, 1339*(1), 154–164. doi:10.1111/nyas.12606.

7 Why psychology is not (yet) a science

Bernhard Hommel

1 Introduction

The concept of science captures knowledge from "the careful study of the structure and behaviour of the physical world, especially by watching, measuring and doing experiments, and the development of theories to describe the results of these activities," as the Cambridge dictionary puts it. A particularly important ingredient of scientific endeavors is the experimenting. While "watching" and "measuring" is necessary to specify the phenomena that call for scientific understanding, "doing experiments" is key to do what science is supposed to do with these phenomena: to explain how they work. In order to understand how something works, systematic observations under different, tightly controlled conditions (i.e., experimenting) are necessary, because only through this, causal mechanisms can be revealed. All these considerations do not only hold for the classical natural sciences but they also apply to scientific psychology, which since the establishment of the first psychological laboratory by Wilhelm Wundt in Leipzig has defined itself by not only providing post-hoc interpretations of observations but by experimentally testing different interpretations against each other. It is this particular attitude that distinguishes scientific psychology from the older, humanities-based, purely interpretational psychological traditions that, similar to theology or the literature sciences, were more interested in sense-making, in providing coherent narratives to extract the deeper logic of empirical observations. Hence, the establishment of the Wundt lab and many others that followed have paved the way for the development of psychology as a truly scientific discipline.

And yet, I will argue that psychology has not yet managed to live up to its potential. The main reason being that psychology has not yet completed the "Galilean turn" that the traditional natural sciences have completed hundreds of years ago. The first who explained what this turn implies for psychology and who argued that psychology still has to perform it was Kurt Lewin (1930, 1931). Lewin contrasted what he called Aristotelian and Galilean psychology, and argued that the former should be considered as a probably necessary first step, which however is now outdated and should be abandoned and replaced by the Galilean approach. He characterizes the two approaches in various ways, but for our present purposes the most central distinction relates to what counts

DOI: 10.4324/9781003360896-7

as an explanation. The Aristotelian approach consists in classifying observations in increasingly abstract ways, so that classes of observations can be theoretically related to each other. These relations are considered to be representing laws, in the sense that observations of class A are considered to cause observations of class B if B always follows A. Exceptions are not permitted, as Aristotle drew a sharp line between perfect regularity and randomness, and considered only the former a legitimate object of science. Accordingly, the Aristotelian approach heavily relies on statistics, so to tell true from apparent regularity—an emphasis that is still visible in the dominant role of statistics in the present "replication crisis" in psychology and related sciences.

According to the Galilean view, all possible events are physically determined, so that exceptions must be explained by means of the same theoretical approach as regularities. This brings in an entirely different concept of how individual cases and individual variability relate to general causal theory, as the latter can only be considered satisfactory if it can account for the former (Hommel & Colzato, 2017a). Causal mechanisms are thus playing an increasingly important role, so that it is no longer sufficient to observe regular sequences of events. This is because regularities provide information about *that* causality may be involved but not about *how* causality might operate, about *how* the mechanics of a preceding event generates the one that follows. Hence, while the Aristotelian view is satisfied with sorting phenomena into increasingly abstract categories and considers successful sorting equitable to scientific understanding, the Galilean view requires a deeper insight into the mechanistic relationship between cause and effect. It is this move from Aristotelian understanding-through-sorting to understanding how psychological processes generate the empirical phenomena under consideration that academic psychology has yet to make. This is at least the claim that I would like to defend in the following.

2 Selecting explananda

According to Lewin, the strong preference for classifying empirical phenomena that is characterizing the Aristotelian approach is already visible in the way explananda (i.e., the to be-explained phenomena) are selected. Indeed, scientific psychology did not begin to investigate the processes underlying human behavior before dividing them in various ways. First into domains, like cognition, emotion, motivation and social, as if a naturally developing brain would be likely to care about the semantic differences between these concepts and develop different strategies to deal with the corresponding aspects of human behavior. Next into apparently obvious subfunctions, like perception, attention, memory, thinking, emotion, action and more. None of these subdivisions reflects the outcome of systematic research, none of them have been justified based on systematic scientific reasoning or empirical data. It could have been that such research would have revealed systematic differences between the processes underlying the process that generates the perception of external or internal states of affairs on the one hand and of generating and retrieving memories about these affairs on the other, which would have suggested to draw a sharp line between perception and memory. But the opposite was the case: research simply took the apparently self-evident distinctions between functions for granted—presumably for no other reasons that language has developed different words for them (Danziger, 1997), and developed very different ways to investigate them and to theorize about them. Only to ask, more than 100 years later, how processes from one domain might affect processes from the other—falsely assuming that labeling a process cognitive, say, precludes that this process is affective or motivational or social at the same time (Hommel, 2019a).

Aristotelian logic did not stop here: Each type of processes was further subdivided (e.g., perceptual processes according to their modality; memory processes according to their stability over time; thinking processes according to their rationality), even though other distinctions would have been possible and not making any distinction might have facilitated the discovery of commonalities. Particularly advanced is this urge to classify with respect to attention, which is further subdivided according to the modality of the attended stimuli, the physical dimension being attended, the external or internal focus of attention, the task-specific function of attentional processes, like suppressing distractions or monitoring a scene over long time, and more (Hommel et al., 2019). The more research was devoted to a particular psychological phenomenon, the more subdivisions were being made and the more distinctions were developed (Hommel & Colzato, 2015). The ineffective consequence of this approach is that the social networks of the researchers carrying out this research follow the same classification logic, so that researchers interested in auditory-spatial exogenous attention are increasingly unlikely to meet colleagues interested in visual vigilance, say, in conferences and symposia, and increasingly unlikely to publish in the same journals. As a logical consequence, very similar theories were developed in parallel, like for instance models of serial action in the areas of motor control and speech production, without any points of contact or mutual recognition.

3 Constructing explanantia

The strong tendency to classify is not only a problem for the definition of the explananda that psychological theory aims to explain, but also for the development of the explanantia (i.e., the explanations themselves). Again, even though scientific articles that promise a better understanding of the causal mechanisms underlying psychological phenomena appear on a daily basis, the entire discipline shows hardly any ambition to really get at causal mechanisms (Hommel, 2020a). Instead, theory building in psychology commonly follows a kind of reification logic. This logic is particularly dominant in personality psychology but can also be seen, at a lower level, in other psychological domains. The idea is that behavior is explained by the characteristics of the person showing it, which in turn are derived from behavior the type of which conceptually overlaps with the one being investigated. Recent studies on conspiracy theories show this tendency very clearly:

studies try to explain the fact that some people are strongly attracted by conspiracy theories (the explanandum) by assuming that these people belong to a special category of individuals who believe in conspiracy theories (the explanans). More specifically, some authors emphasize that the tendency to adopt conspiracy theories is systematically related to particular personality traits, like the motivation for sense-making and paranormal belief, or particular combinations of the so-called "big five" personality factors (for an overview, see Goreis & Voracek, 2019). Given that neither these factors nor the more specific traits and motivations they are statistically associated with are already understood with respect to their mechanistic basis, this theoretical strategy consists in nothing but *empirical generalization* (people who do this also do similar other things) plus *sorting*: people engage in conspiracy theories because they are this kind of people that tend to engage in this kind of stuff. What it means to be this kind of people and why it is this kind of stuff they tend to engage in remains entirely unclear. Hence, the theoretical strategy consists in taking an explanandum, an observed behavior that one intends to explain, reifying it, and projecting it into the person showing this behavior, and then taking this projection as an explanation.

Reification strategies are particularly popular in psychological approaches to social phenomena. If an individual shows racist behavior, say, this is explained by the racist attitude the person must have had (people show racist behavior because they are racists). This might be acceptable if we had good mechanistic theories explaining where attitudes come from and how they are represented, and how they affect and drive behavior. But not only are these theories lacking, there is also strong evidence that at least many kinds of attitudes are unable to predict behavior—also known as the attitude–behavior gap (e.g., Kollmuss & Agyeman, 2002). Hence, what remains is the practice to take an explanandum, project it into the mind of the individual, and then considering this projection an explanans. Reification also dominates at the groups or systems level, where the observation of racist behavior has been attributed to "systemic racism," which in turn has been defined by NAACP President Derrick Johnson as "systems and structures that have procedures or processes that disadvantages African Americans." The explanation of racial behavior through systemic racism would have theoretical content if we had a good idea regarding the workings of these hypothetical "systems and structures," regarding which exact "procedures or processes" might be responsible, regarding where the racism infecting the systems and structures was coming from and how it mechanistically managed to modify the procedures and processes. But nothing of that we have which, as pointed out by Lutz (2022), renders the explanation of racist behavior by systemic racism completely tautological.

The same theoretical strategy is dominating the cognitive neurosciences. For instance, the fascinating human ability to put oneself into the shoes of others (empathy, theory of mind) has been extensively studied by means of various kinds of neurocognitive machinery, such as EEG and fMRI. The empirical strategy typically consists in having participants engage in tasks that require the use of this skill and in tasks that do not, and then measure which brain area is more active in the former condition than in the latter. In the case of theory of mind, it is especially the right temporal-parietal junction (rTPJ) that covariates with the degree to which theory of mind is required in a task, which indeed was taken to fully explain the skill (Saxe, Carey & Kanwisher, 2004). That is, the mere having of a particular system that, because of its covarying activation is assumed to do whatever the cognitive skill under investigation might be doing, is sufficient to explain the behavior of interest.

On the one hand, it is certainly important to study to which degree brain areas or processes in the brain are engaged in, and important for a particular behavior and the underlying skill. On the other hand, however, this can only be a first step to unravel the true mechanism. Because the mere having of a brain part that contributes to a particular behavior is theoretically trivial: cognitive neuroscientists should be truly worried if no such part could be identified. But why this particular area, this particular system? Does it have a particular computational ability, house a particular type of neurons that can do things that other areas of neurons can't do? Does it have or connect to or interact with particularly interesting neighbors that, together, can generate behavior that other interactions cannot? Or does it perhaps emerge at a particularly interesting point in time of the ontogenetic neural development, where particular other systems exist already while others are yet to emerge? Hence, why is it the rTPJ and not any other system that is so important for our theory of mind? And, most importantly, exactly how does the rTPJ manage to generate theory of mind? Answers to these questions would require at least some idea about how theory of mind works, but they would also pay back by providing interesting constraints for understanding exactly these workings. And yet, almost no one is asking these questions. Apparently, because sorting seems enough.

Reification is also used at an even lower functional level. For instance, cognitive psychology was, and in some parts still is dominated by the so-called stage approach originally developed by Donders (1868) and later methodologically fine-tuned by Sternberg (1969). The idea is that the psychological processes starting with the registration of a stimulus at a sensory surface and ending with the execution of a response to that stimulus can be subdivided into meaningful processing stages. A typical subdivision includes stages labeled as "sensory processing," "perception," "decision-making/response-selection," and "motor performance," or similar, plus possible extra stages that may or may not share capacity with the stages, or intervene between them. A given phenomenon is considered to be fully and satisfactorily explained if it can be assigned to one particular stage or a combination of particular stages. For instance, research on multitasking over more than 90 years reported in far more than 1000 articles was devoted to the question which particular processing stage is responsible for our obvious difficulty to carry out more than one task at a time (Pashler, 1994). Ironically, the eventual, now widely accepted answer is that this is likely to be the response-selection stage— which was already the best bet of one of the first systematic experimental articles on this issue (Telford, 1931).

The problematic aspect of this gigantic quest is not that it took so long and that its outcome is so meager. All this might indicate the care and depth devoted to solidify a scientific claim. Rather, the problem is that the widespread agreement on how this particular phenomenon should be sorted in the stage-theoretical toolbox is considered to be fully satisfactory—even though no one knows exactly how the hypothetical stages might operate. All stages are defined by a particular function, such as selecting a particular response, which was not theoretically inferred or justified, but simply made up ad hoc by researchers after some armchair reasoning. But how exactly the different stages might be achieving their function, how stimuli are perceived, how responses are selected, is as unknown as the mechanistic reason for why multiple stimuli can be selected concurrently while responses cannot. What is it about stimulus representations and response representations that is responsible for this obvious difference? We don't know. Worse, no one is even asking! Hence, Aristotelian sorting demarcates the goal and endpoint of the scientific quest, and no truly mechanistic curiosity follows.

A final example for the supremacy of Aristotelian thinking in our current theorizing comes from studies of human rationality and thought processes. Particularly popular in this field are approaches that distinguish between two systems that people are assumed to use when making decisions (Evans, 2003). System 1, as it is often called, is considered to be dumb but fast and effortless, while System 2 is believed to be smart but slow and effortful (Stanovich & West, 2000). The inner workings of both systems remain more or less a mystery, apart from assumptions that System 1 is "associative," while System 2 is "rule-based"—which neglects the fact that the associative nature of the human brain must generate even rule-based thinking in an associative way, and that associative systems can easily represent rules and show rule-based behavior (e.g., Hunt, 1989). Research based on the assumption of these two systems proceeds in the classical Aristotelian fashion: every sign of a lack of rationality, whether this is defined in terms of logicality or personal utility (Evans, Over & Manktelow, 1993), is assumed to represent a contribution of System 1, whereas every positive sign of rationality is attributed to System 2. Again, this comes down to the projection of the scientific concepts of rationality on the one hand and irrationality on the other into the head of the individual, and to engage in circular theorizing: whatever is rational is explained by the activity of the rational system and whatever is irrational is explained by the activity of the irrational system.

It is true that some ideas have been developed and tested under which circumstances System 2 might contribute less, such as when under stress or when occupied by other tasks, but exactly how these two systems work we still don't know. If there were more interest in the actual mechanisms of both systems, it would be easier to judge whether they really differ in terms of the processes they make use of, the codes they consider, and the processing style they can be characterized by. This in turn would be important for distinguishing between the two systems approach and multiple other interpretations of the available findings. For instance, many findings do not so much seem to imply two different processing styles but, rather, the presence or absence of one additional process. Take, for instance, a classical question often used to demonstrate people's lack of rationality: "A bat and a ball cost $1.10 in total. The bat costs $1.00 more than the ball. How much does the ball cost?" While the correct answer would be $0.05, many people, including college students, tend to answer $0.10. As pointed out by Kahneman (2011) and others, the difference between a wrong and right answer is one additional checking operation: even if I tend to think of $0.10 as a possible answer, checking it by adding up the two amounts would give a cost of $1.20, which would indicate that the answer must be wrong. Now, if the difference between wrong and right and, thus, between intuitive and rational, consists in one additional cognitive operation, we don't need to assume an entirely different system to account for this difference. Indeed, providing feedback about the mistake and explaining that additional checking would have prevented it is likely to help avoiding the error in the future. Hence, people may simply need to learn when to recheck their answers, which might be done by the exact same system that has produced them in the first place. More theoretical interest in the actual mechanism would help to test this and other possibilities.

4. Metapsychological considerations

As I have argued, the current zeitgeist of psychological theorizing is still penetrated by Aristotelian thinking. Before addressing the question how we could promote a Galilean turn of scientific psychology, let us briefly consider possible reasons for why Aristotelian thinking is still so popular. Addressing this question would benefit from systematic research on how researchers theorize in general and how they do so in psychology in particular. Unfortunately, such a kind of metapsychology has not yet been established and I am not aware of systematic data that provide a sufficiently solid empirical basis for a comprehensive approach. Nevertheless, I can imagine that the following three factors play an important role in preventing the psychological sciences to take the next step.

The first two factors are tightly related to the fact that psychology differs from almost all other scientific disciplines with respect to the fact that researchers are agents and subjects of the research at the same time. A natural scientist analyzing the structure of snowflakes, say, may have strong affection towards the object of her studies, but her scientific perspective and objectivity is unlikely to be clouded by particular similarities between her and the object under investigation. This is different for psychologists: almost everything we can say about the object/subject of our studies also applies to ourselves and to our personal social environment. This is likely to have consequences. For instance, Braitenberg (1984) has pointed out that researchers tend to generate substantial theoretical overhead when trying to understand the underpinnings of human behavior. Whereas simplistic models and theories are very welcome when explaining the behavior of non-human animals or artificial agents, any human-like feature that even geometric symbols might be taken to exhibit seems to elicit the strong tendency in human observers, researchers included, to interpret events in terms of intentions and reasons (Heider & Simmel, 1944).

With respect to humans as subjects of psychological research, this is an interesting empirical observation that calls for an explanation. With respect to humans as agents of psychological research, however, this can be considered a counterproductive clinging to our roots in the humanities. Theorizing in the humanities commonly consists in sense-making by interpreting empirical events in terms of the reasons that the respective agents may have had. The sciences, however, are rather interested in the causes of phenomena, in the causal mechanisms that were technically generating them. For the understanding of these mechanisms, reasoning-based interpretations are commonly not very useful. Hence, if mechanistic theorizing about the friendly behavior of a daycare robot is calling for a chain of events consisting in defined processes operating on defined informational codes rather than an account in terms of the possible motives and emotions that the robot might have had, it does not seem to be scientifically acceptable to use the opposite criteria when trying to explain the mechanisms underlying human behavior. And yet, given that this is exactly how we proceed in our discipline, the fact that we always are agents and subjects of our research at the same time seems to stand in the way of mechanistic thinking.

This dual relationship of ourselves to our research also relates to the second factor that I consider important: the preoccupation with conscious experience. In the pre-academic phase of psychological theorizing, all our data necessarily came from our conscious experience. This implies two kinds of limitations. First, it does not allow us to assess processes and codes that are either usually running outside of conscious experience or that may even be inaccessible to conscious experience however hard we try. Even researchers interested in thinking admit that 90% or more of the interesting drivers of our thinking and acting are not available to conscious experience (e.g., Kahneman, 2011), which is really a lot. But there is a second limitation. As we know since James (1890) and others, all we can hope to perceive consciously is the outcomes of the psychological processes of interest. While it is not impossible that products are telling us something about the way they were produced, there is no 1:1 process-product relationship and it is also hard to characterize a process if it cannot be monitored in principle. Hence, if mechanistic theorizing requires ideas about how processes operate on codes to generate a particular psychological outcome, there is almost nothing of what a mechanistic theory needs to include that even the scientifically most educated conscious awareness can deliver. A good example in case is the psychology of thinking, which is very rich in ideas about what kind of information people may consider when making what kinds of decisions, but extremely poor if it comes to mechanistic scenarios explaining how we actually think. The possible reason for this ignorance is likely to do with the fact that we, as scientists, can think for ourselves, and so we do not consider that as a problem that would require any further explanation. And yet, I'm afraid it does.

A third factor that seems to play a role in preventing a Galilean turn consists in the fact that by far the most phenomena that psychologists are busy with can be considered social constructions or at least reflections of the way we organize our social behavior. A perhaps obvious example is research on conformity. This research was initiated by Asch in the 1950s, where many societies showed many signs of conformity, even the more individualistic Western democracies, like the United States. But now, more than 70 years later, individualism has progressed very substantially, and so it does not seem surprising that the sizes of conformity effects were found to decay over time (Bond & Smith, 1996). Hence, it may very well be that there won't be any measurable conformity effects in the near future. The same goes for many other social phenomena, just think of stereotyping, which is likely to become more realistic (i.e., less "stereotypic") with increasing information about other cultures and subcultures available through the Internet, the impact of social norms, interpersonal perception, or moral reasoning. Social constructivists have argued that this dependency of psychological phenomena on culture questions the value of empirical research and our present approach of seeking for empirical verification/falsification in controlled studies that draw a distinction between the agent and the subject of research (e.g., Gergen, 1985). I do not share this negative assessment, but it is certainly true that the regularities in human behavior that psychological theorizing tries to explain are unlikely to reflect context-independent laws but rather seem to be social constructions that can vary with the cultural context.

The present custom to rely on empirical generalization (Fiedler, 1991), rather than true theorizing, when trying to explain human behavior does not leave us well-equipped to meet this challenge. Empirical generalization takes an observation, such as longer reaction times if one is to name the blue color of a stimulus that consists of the letters RED (rather than BLUE; aka the Stroop effect), tests whether this observation can be generalized to other kinds of stimuli and responses (e.g., whether naming the number of 3 letters in the letter string 444 vs. 333 also produces longer reaction times) and, if that is the case, reformulates the observation in an abstract fashion. For instance, such an endeavor might lead to the theoretical conclusion that stimuli with multiple dimensions slow down responding if the different dimensions indicate different responses (e.g., Kornblum, Hasbroucq & Osman, 1990). It is certainly important to see how far an effect can be generalized and to reformulate the observation in the most abstract way possible, depending on the empirical support. But why that can be considered a mechanistic explanation is hard to see. After all, if an alien from outer space would land on the earth and try to understand what mechanism allows automobiles to move, she would be unlikely to really understand this mechanism after having generalized the observation to the fact that most boxes with four or more wheels are able to move at different speeds. So why do we fail to continue with our theorizing after having formulated the most abstract version of our observation?

A possible reason might be that scientific researchers believe that human behavior is governed by laws, just like the objects of other scientific disciplines. And there are a few laws indeed, such as Weber's Law in perception and the third power law in movement control. But not many more. This, together with the mentioned cultural dependency of many psychological phenomena, suggests that most of the human behavior we are interested in is not governed by laws in the actual sense and, thus, are unlikely to be well captured by empirical generalization. One may argue that this only holds for phenomena that are obviously social in character, but not for more basic processes. And yet, even basic processes depend on culture. For instance, inspired by the cultural studies on perception of Nisbett and colleagues, colleagues and I investigated other basic psychological processes in members of cultural subgroups that are likely to differ in terms of individualism versus collectivism. For instance, religions differ substantially with respect to their emphasis on individualistic versus collectivistic goals and values, which may affect the way they perceive, attend to, decide upon, and act on stimulus events (Hommel & Colzato, 2010). Indeed, members of individualistic religions turned out to show significantly better performance than non-religious individuals or members of collectivistic religions in tasks that require patience or the focusing on relevant and the ignoring of task-irrelevant information, but to show significantly worse performance in tasks requiring the integration of information over time and space (Hommel & Colzato, 2017b). Similar findings were obtained for different kinds of sexual orientation (Colzato et al., 2010). Given that we used tasks that were constructed to assess basic mechanisms of human information processing, this suggests that almost all phenomena in the psychological sciences might be sensitive to cultural factors. If so, this poses two challenges to psychological theory: For one, most psychological phenomena are not simply due to "a given," a psychological law that requires and deserves no further mechanistic consideration. For another, even theories on the simplest psychological processes are unlikely to really hold if they do not contain mechanistic details that can account for cultural and other kinds of variability.

5. Towards a Galilean turn

So far, I have argued that the discipline of psychology still has a long way to go to become a true science. According to Lewin (1930, 1931), taking a Galilean turn would be an important milestone on this way. But given the continuing popularity of Aristotelian thinking in psychology, this turn does not seem to be a natural developmental step in the growth of our scientific discipline. So how can we push this development? How can we become more Galilean? How can we become interested in psychological and neurocognitive mechanisms in a truly mechanistic sense, and versed in using ideas about such mechanisms to inform our empirical research? Some hints towards a Galilean therapy are already provided in Lewin's diagnostic papers, but I also think that specific therapeutic interventions to overcome our tendency to generate tautological projections into the heads of the agent that we study might be useful. So, what follows are two suggestions how to increase the Galilean flavor of our theoretical thinking.

5.1 *From binary to continuous theorizing*

A natural move to overcome Aristotelian sorting logic consists in transforming category systems into continua or multidimensional spaces. This is particularly easy with binary categories, which are abundant in Aristotelian thinking anyway. For instance, the clinical sciences could easily admit that the distinctions between typical and atypical, between healthy and ill, are not as rigid and qualitative as the binary terms sound. Psychiatric/clinical categories almost never refer to one particular feature, and rarely to features that are binary in nature. In practice, this means that almost all features and characteristics that psychiatrically diagnosed patients exhibit are shared by many individuals that are considered to be psychiatrically healthy. In other words, the feature distributions of psychiatrically typical and atypical individuals overlap to a large degree, which is true for almost any feature one may think of. Accordingly, a continuous approach would be both scientifically and practically more logical, with the positive side effect of reducing the stigmatization of patients (Hommel & Beste, 2021). More continuous views have also been suggested in other domains and areas, such as the distinction between intentional and automatic processes (Hommel, 2019b) or the social construction of gender (Morgenroth & Ryan, 2018).

Apart from the fact that assuming a continuum rather than discrete categories may often be more realistic, continuous views are also likely to stimulate more theoretical creativity and indeed more interest in psychological and neurocognitive mechanisms. The reason is that a continuous view naturally attracts attention to intra-individual and inter-individual variability. In the Aristotelian view, variability is equivalent with noise, which is equivalent with chaos, which cannot be considered in science by (his) definition. According to the Galilean view, however, the world is completely deterministic, so that even deviance, variability, and noise can be and must be scientifically accounted for. With binary categories as the key theoretical concepts, noise within each category must be considered noise in an Aristotelian sense or measurement error, as the popular statistical approaches suggest. With continua, however, variability even among individuals or behaviors that are considered to be categorially equivalent becomes theoretically interesting and challenging. Because the Galilean ambition would need to be that both means and variability must be accounted for by means of the same theory, by means of the same mechanisms. Hence, a Galilean view would suggest developing unitary theories that are sufficiently flexible to cover the whole empirical continuum, so to explain both typicality and atypicality, and to explain both intentional and automatic processes by means of the same mechanistic model.

A more continuous view would also change our interpretation of replications and failures to replicate. In the current discussion of the so-called "replication crisis" in psychology, the scientific status of replications has been strongly promoted. This is certainly a useful development, but the discussion is often restricted to the overly binary question whether a particular effect does or does not exist. This overlooks the fact that much of the neurocognitive software that implements the mechanisms we are interested in is a product of culture and, therefore, likely to depend on the cultural context and to change over time—as already discussed. Interestingly, this dependency is entirely overlooked in the recent replication efforts. Not being able to find an effect that was previously reported from another lab (often in another country with other cultural habits and religious convictions) is taken to imply that the effect is not "real," rather than as an indication of a possible context dependency that calls for further research and further theorizing. Hence, while the present Aristotelian interpretation of failures to replicate is focusing on statistics, and on the distinction between signal and (statistical) "noise," a Galilean turn would emphasize the role of theory and help to develop increasingly complex theories that take on board increasingly complex context-dependencies.

5.2 *From analytic to synthetic theorizing*

The distinction between analytic and synthetic theory building has been introduced by Braitenberg (1984). As already mentioned, he pointed out that theorizing about human behavior often generates theoretical overhead, due to the overly rich interpretation and the assumed contribution of inner "reasons" of agents that are driving their behavior. As a cure to avoid such overhead, Braitenberg suggests a synthetic approach that tries to reconstruct phenomena by combining theoretically well-understood, transparent mechanisms, rather than by inventing novel constructs with unclear semantic fields. Classical behaviorism in some sense has promoted a similar view, by restricting the theorizing to very few learning-related constructs. It seems clear that the allergy of behaviorism to internal states and representations stood in the way of a broader success of this endeavor. However, there is no reason to shy away from internal codes and processes when trying to reconstruct psychological phenomenon.

For instance, I have tried to show that basic mechanisms (codes, processes and interactions between them) taken from the theory of event coding (Hommel et al., 2001), which was originally developed to account for interactions between perception and action, can easily account for other phenomena far outside the envisioned range of the original theory (e.g., Hommel, 2021; Hommel & Stevenson, 2021; Kim & Hommel, 2015). Along the same lines, Frings et al. (2020) have argued that the basic elements of the theory of event coding seem very suitable to account for observations from various areas of research, ranging from perception to attention, memory and learning, and probably even social phenomena. Hence, synthetic theorizing about internal processes is possible, and making use of a restricted sets of theoretical elements and tools would strongly facilitate the construction of unitary, comprehensive theories that can account for phenomena from various strands of research (Hommel & Wiers, 2017).

Interestingly, the synthetic approach is consistent with Feynman's famous dictum "What I cannot create, I do not understand." To create something, whether in terms of functionality or actual hardware, presupposes the sufficient understanding of the actual mechanics. Building a car requires more than assuming that cars move because of their intentions and their abilities to do so. It requires the basic understanding of the concept of an engine, of fuel, of the creation of motion through explosion or other means, and the transmission of such motion to wheels that show some resistance to the surface. These concepts do not need to be replicated 1:1 to make for a good model of the mechanism, but they need to be understood in greater detail than current theories of the human mind and brain provide about the phenomena they intend to explain. And assumptions about these detailed mechanisms need to be tested against the way nature constructs the respective psychological phenomena, be it through the analysis of developmental processes or the experimental creation of new phenomena (e.g., a novel kind of motivation or emotion, or a novel kind of cognitive mechanism) according to the same mechanistic principles.

However, it is important to realize that the promotion of synthetic theorizing would call for a culture change in the reviewing process. Current theorizing strongly suffers from what has been called the toothbrush problem (Mischel, 2008): using theories of others is commonly taken as a lack of originality and intellectual autonomy, rather than an optimal service to Occam's razor. Likewise, applying theories to phenomena other than they were developed for is commonly considered a logical mistake rather than an exciting intellectual and empirical endeavor. Accordingly, the promotion of synthetic theorizing will require an effective campaign to establish theoretical parsimony as an important virtue in our publication system.

6 Conclusion

I have argued that the psychological and the neurocognitive sciences are way too under ambitious with respect to the mechanisms underlying human behavior. Once we have engaged in several cycles of empirical generalization, we take the abstract redescription of the corresponding phenomena as a kind of psychological law and as a fully satisfactory explanation of the phenomenon. I suggest that this is not enough. More specifically, I consider this a strong indication that we are still stuck in what Lewin has considered the Aristotelian phase of psychology, and that it is high time to move forward. To realize the needed Galilean turn, we need to develop a more scientifically fruitful way to deal with our twofold occupation with human behavior as the agent and subject of our own research. It may also be helpful to train ourselves turning the binary theorizing that is so characteristic of almost all fields of current psychology and the clinical sciences into a more continuous theoretical format. And to take noise, interindividual and intraindividual variability more seriously and try considering it more openly and more explicitly in our theorizing. Finally, a useful therapeutical move might be to engage more in synthetic reconstruction of psychological phenomena, rather than in the typical top-down segmentation of phenomena into smaller and smaller pieces, with increasing distance to the phenomena of interest.

Acknowledgements

This research was supported by a Double-100 Talent Grant of the Province of Shandong, China to the author.

References

Bond, R. & Smith, P. B. (1996). Culture and conformity: A meta-analysis of studies using Asch's (1952b, 1956) line judgment task. *Psychological Bulletin*, 119, 111–137.

Braitenberg, V. (1984). *Vehicles: Experiments in synthetic psychology*. MIT Press.

Colzato, L. S., van Hooidonk, L., van den Wildenberg, W. P. M., Harinck, F. & Hommel, B. (2010). Sexual orientation biases attentional control: a possible gaydar mechanism. *Frontiers in Psychology*, 1, 13.

Danziger, K. (1997). *Naming the mind: How psychology found its language*. Sage.

Donders, F. C. (1868). Over de snelheid van psychische processen. *Onderzoekingen gedaan in het Physiologisch Laboratorium der Utrechtsche Hoogeschool (1968–1869)*, 2, 92–120.

Evans, J. S. B. T. (2003). In two minds: Dual-process accounts of reasoning. *Trends in Cognitive Sciences*, 7, 454–459.

Evans, J. S., Over, D. E. & Manktelow, K. I. (1993). Reasoning, decision making and rationality. *Cognition*, 49, 165–187.

Fiedler, K. (1991). Heuristic biases in theory formation: On the cognitive processes of those concerned with cognitive processes. *Theory & Psychology*, 1, 407–430.

Frings, C., *et al.* (2020). Binding and retrieval in action control (BRAC). *Trends in Cognitive Sciences*, 24, 375–387.

Gergen, K. J. (1985). The social constructionist movement in modern psychology. *American Psychologist*, 40, 266–275.

Goreis, A. & Voracek, M. (2019). A systematic review and meta-analysis of psychological research on conspiracy beliefs: Field characteristics, measurement instruments, and associations with personality traits. *Frontiers in Psychology*, 10, 205.

Heider, F. & Simmel, M. (1944). An experimental study of apparent behavior. *American Journal of Psychology*, 57, 243–259.

Hommel, B. (2019a). Affect and control: A conceptual clarification. *International Journal of Psychophysiology*, 144, 1–6.

Hommel, B. (2019b). Binary theorizing doesn't account for action control. *Frontiers in Psychology*, 10, 2542.

Hommel, B. (2020a). Pseudo-mechanistic explanations in psychology and cognitive neuroscience. *Topics in Cognitive Science*, 12, 1294–1305.

Hommel, B. (2020b). Dual-task performance: Theoretical analysis and an event-coding account. *Journal of Cognition*, 3(1), 29.

Hommel, B. (2021). The Me-file: An event-coding approach to self-representation. *Frontiers in Psychology*, 10, 3389.

Hommel, B. & Beste, C. (2021). Towards an ideology-free, truly mechanistic health psychology. *International Journal of Environmental Research and Public Health*, 18 (21), 11126.

Hommel, B., Chapman, C. S., Cisek, P., Neyedli, H. F., Song, J.-H. & Welsh, T. N. (2019). No one knows what attention is. *Attention, Perception & Psychophysics*, 81, 2288–2303.

Hommel, B. & Colzato, L. S. (2010). Religion as a control guide: on the impact of religion on cognition. *Zygon: Journal of Religion & Science*, 45, 596–604.

Hommel, B. & Colzato, L. S. (2015). Learning from history: The need for a synthetic approach to human cognition. *Frontiers in Psychology*, 6, 1435.

Hommel, B. & Colzato, L. S. (2017a). The grand challenge: Integrating nomothetic and ideographic approaches to human cognition. *Frontiers in Psychology*, 8, 100.

Hommel, B. & Colzato, L. S. (2017b). The social transmission of metacontrol policies: Mechanisms underlying the interpersonal transfer of persistence and flexibility. *Neuroscience and Biobehavioral Reviews*, 81, 43–58.

Hommel, B., Müsseler, J., Aschersleben, G. & Prinz, W. (2001). The theory of event coding (TEC): A framework for perception and action planning. *Behavioral and Brain Sciences*, 24, 849–878.

Hommel, B. & Stevenson, N. (2021). An event-coding account of attitudes. *Psychonomic Bulletin & Review*, 28, 2057–2063.

Hommel, B. & Wiers, R. W. (2017). Towards a unitary approach to human action control. *Trends in Cognitive Sciences*, 21, 940–949.

Hunt, E. (1989). Connectionist and rule-based representations of expert knowledge. *Behavior Research Methods, Instruments & Computers*, 21, 88–95.

James, W. (1890). *The principles of psychology*. Macmillan.

Kahneman, D. (2011). *Thinking, fast and slow*. Macmillan.

Kim, D. & Hommel, B. (2015). An event-based account of conformity. *Psychological Science*, 26, 484–489.

Kollmuss, A. & Agyeman, J. (2002). Mind the Gap: Why do people act environmentally and what are the barriers to pro-environmental behavior? *Environmental Education Research*, 8, 239–260.

Kornblum, S., Hasbroucq, T. & Osman, A. (1990). Dimensional overlap: Cognitive basis for stimulus-response compatibility—a model and taxonomy. *Psychological Review*, 97, 253–270.

Lewin, K. (1930). Der Übergang von der aristotelischen zur galileischen Denkweise in Biologie und Psychologie. *Erkenntnis*, 1, 421–466.

Lewin, K. (1931). The conflict between Aristotelian and Galilean modes of thought in contemporary psychology. *Journal of General Psychology*, 5, 141–176.

Lutz, M. (2022). The problem with "systemic racism". Retrieved from www.persuasion.community/p/the-problem-with-systemic-racism.

Mischel, W. (2008). The toothbrush problem. Retrieved from www.psychologicalscience.org/observer/the-toothbrush-problem.

Morgenroth, T. & Ryan, M. K. (2018). Gender trouble in social psychology: How can Butler's work inform experimental social psychologists' conceptualization of gender? *Frontiers in Psychology*, 9, 1320.

Pashler, H. (1994). Dual-task interference in simple tasks: Data and theory. *Psychological Bulletin*, 116, 220–244.

Saxe, R., Carey, S. & Kanwisher, N. (2004). Understanding other minds: Linking developmental psychology and functional neuroimaging. *Annual Review of Psychology*, 55, 87–124.

Stanovich, K. & West, R. (2000). Individual differences in reasoning: Implications for the rationality debate? *Behavioral and Brain Sciences*, 23, 645–665.

Sternberg, S. (1969). The discovery of processing stages: Extensions of Donders' method. *Acta Psychologica*, 30, 276–315.

Telford, C. W. (1931). The refractory phase of voluntary and associative responses. *Journal of Experimental Psychology*, 14, 1–36.

Index

FSC
www.fsc.org
MIX
Papier | Fördert
gute Waldnutzung
FSC® C083411

Kolibri 360 GmbH
Ferdinand-Jühlke-Straße 7
99095 Erfurt, Deutschland
produktsicherheit@kolibri360.de